The Owl

THE OWL

A Biography

Stephen Moss

 SQUARE PEG

3 5 7 9 10 8 6 4 2

Square Peg, an imprint of Vintage, is part of the Penguin Random House group of
companies whose addresses can be found at global.penguinrandomhouse.com

Penguin
Random House
UK

First published by Square Peg in 2023

penguin.co.uk/vintage

Printed and bound in Latvia by Livonia Print

The authorised representative in the EEA is Penguin Random House Ireland,
Morrison Chambers, 32 Nassau Street, Dublin D02 YH68

A CIP catalogue record for this book is available from the British Library

ISBN 9781529908268

Penguin Random House is committed to a sustainable
future for our business, our readers and our planet. This book
is made from Forest Stewardship Council® certified paper.

To Kevin and Donna Cox: hands-on conservationists,
generous hosts and dear friends

Contents

PROLOGUE

A wise old owl lived in an oak
The more he saw the less he spoke
The less he spoke the more he heard.
Why can't we all be like that wise old bird?

Anonymous

Any encounter with an owl, at any time of the day or night, is always unforgettable.

The tawny owl, hooting loudly outside my home – in the middle of an autumn morning.

The barn owl, floating silently alongside me as I cycled home from a night at the local pub.

The little owl, calling so loudly from our rooftop at night that it kept my teenage son awake.

The short-eared owl, piercing yellow eyes staring back at me one snowy Christmas Eve: the only living bird I saw on my walk.

The long-eared owl, materialising out of a thick hawthorn hedgerow on a hot, bright August day, to be instantly mobbed by a flock of angry swallows.

The snowy owl, the last resident of its kind in Britain – and the only one I have ever seen – hunched down on a rocky hillside on the Shetland island of Fetlar, more than forty years ago.

And a female eagle owl – the largest member of its family in Europe – sitting on its nest like a contented cat, on a cliff face in Hungary's Zemplen Hills.

I can remember every single one of these brief encounters – and virtually every other time I have seen an owl – for one simple reason.

Owls are so elusive, so enigmatic – and just so hard to find – that whenever we chance upon one, the moment always stays in our memory.

But although we don't see owls very often, we do *hear* them. Indeed, since sound is the primary form of communication for most species of owl, hearing one call is in many ways more significant than a fleeting glimpse.

For our forest-dwelling ancestors, the call of the tawny owl would have been part of the soundtrack to their lives, from autumn, through the cold winter months, and well into the following spring. When human beings first settled down to farm the land, they would have heard the discordant shrieking of the bird they knew as the 'screech owl', and we now call the barn owl, at dusk, and through the night. This jarring noise, along with the bird's ghostly-pale plumage, led to the barn owl's association with tales of spirits of long-dead souls risen from the grave.

WHITE OR BARN-OWL ⅟₁

Owls are, by a long way, the most mysterious of all the world's birds. Much, though not quite all, of this mystery is down to the fact that many of them only emerge at night – or at dawn and dusk – and so live in an ethereal, unknowable world far removed from our own, day-bound existence. 'Owls inhabit the one landscape that we weak-sighted, day-loving primates still haven't mastered,' writes the naturalist and author Mark Cocker: 'Night-time.'

As Reginald Bosworth Smith wrote in his 1905 book *Bird Life and Bird Lore*:

> There is no bird which, in its strange and solitary character, its weird and hollow cries, the grotesque solemnity of its appearance, the time-honoured beliefs and superstitions which cluster round it, the large part it has played in poetry, ancient and modern, as well as its sister arts, sculpture and painting, the marvellous adaptations of its structure to its mode of life, or its mode of life to its structure . . . possesses so peculiar a fascination . . . as the various species of owl.

But there is more to our unavoidable fascination with owls. When you look directly at an owl, it appears to be staring straight back at you. That is because, unlike most other birds, they have their eyes on the front of their face, rather than at the sides, giving them binocular vision – just like us. It also, of course, gives them a very human appearance.

Since the beginnings of our civilisation, encounters with owls have given rise to more superstitions, myths and legends than any other group of birds. Owls are associated with wisdom ('the wise old owl'), and are considered to hoot to ward off evil; at the same time, in many parts of sub-Saharan Africa owls are linked with sorcery, and as a consequence often persecuted.

The reality, though, is as improbable as the myth. Owls' largely nocturnal lifestyle has seen them evolve a suite of unique characteristics and behaviours. The barn owl, for example, has incredibly soft feathering, allowing it to float over meadows without voles or mice being able to hear it approach. Like most owls, it has asymmetrical ears – one positioned slightly higher than the other – enabling it to pinpoint the exact whereabouts of its target, hiding somewhere in the grass below.

There are close to 250 different species of owl, in every continent apart from Antarctica. Just seven of these can be seen in Britain (out of sixteen species found in Europe as a whole), but these 'magnificent seven' – tawny, little, barn, short-eared, long-eared, snowy and eagle owls – are among the best-known in the world. Scientists have studied them by night and by day, while amateur naturalists and writers, from Gilbert White and John Clare to a host of modern 'new nature writers', have added a further trove of remarkable tales.

I have seen all five British breeding species of owl – tawny, barn, little, short-eared and long-eared – many times; the snowy owl, just once; and although I have never seen the newcomer, the eagle owl, in Britain, I have watched this huge and fearsome bird a number of times abroad.

I have had many memorable encounters with owls around the world, too: the tiny pygmy owl in Sweden, the huge great grey owl in Belarus, the burrowing owl in Florida, Pel's fishing owl in Botswana's Okavango Delta, and many more (see Chapter 9).

I hope that you, too, will have had your own encounters with owls; all the more unforgettable because they are often so frustratingly brief. Whether a tawny owl calling in a city park, a barn owl drifting at dusk across a grassy field, or a plump little owl perched in an oak tree, looking more like a Russian doll than a bird, these are moments you will remember for ever.

For the quartet of biographies of British birds I've written so far – the *Robin*, *Wren*, *Swallow* and *Swan* – I chose our most popular species. Now I'm turning my attention to a group of birds we hardly ever see, and only occasionally hear, but which nevertheless command our attention to a disproportionate and surprising extent: the owls.

Unlike previous volumes, which have focused on a single species and its life cycle throughout the year, this book covers all seven species of owl that can be regularly seen in the British Isles. These species – along with others, such as the pygmy, scops, Tengmalm's, Ural, hawk and great grey owls – are also found widely across continental Europe, though they may be just as difficult to find there as well!

Throughout the book, I shall examine, and try to provide answers to, the key paradox about owls: that they are both familiar, and yet at the same time enigmatic and unfamiliar.

Tawny Owl	
Average size	Length 37–39 cm, wingspan 99 cm, weight 420–520 gm
Behaviour	Almost entirely nocturnal
Range	Found across much of lowland England, Wales and Scotland, including cities, towns and suburbs as well as the wider countryside. Absent from upland areas, the whole of Ireland, and from most offshore islands apart from Anglesey and the Isle of Wight.
Breeding season	March to July
Eggs	2–3
Incubation period	30 days
Fledging period	35–39 days
Hunting habits	Ambushes prey by dropping down or gliding from perch
Lifespan	Average 4 years
UK population	50,000 pairs
European population	Between one and two million individuals
How to find them	Tawny owls are almost entirely nocturnal, and are usually discovered by listening for their famous *tu-whit, tu-whoo* call (actually a duet between the female and the male). During the day, they might be found at a roost in a large tree, usually when discovered by small birds who mob them noisily. Young tawnies leave the nest before they fledge and may sometimes be seen at daytime, perched together on the branch of a tree.

Barn Owl	
Average size	Length 34 cm, wingspan 89 cm, weight 300–360 gm
Behaviour	Crepuscular (seen at dawn or dusk) and nocturnal
Range	Found in rural parts of farmed lowland England, Wales, southern Scotland, and Ireland, though often in fairly low numbers. Absent from towns, cities and upland areas.
Breeding season	April to July
Eggs	4–6
Incubation period	32 days
Fledging period	53–61 days
Hunting habits	Flies low over open, grassy areas before dropping down onto prey
Lifespan	Average 4 years
UK population	10,000 to 12,000 pairs
European population	Between 110,000 and 230,000 pairs
How to find them	Barn owls do fly at night, but your best chance to see one is at dawn or dusk, when the light is low enough to hunt but bright enough for you to see them. They fly low over grassy fields, heaths and wetlands, often quartering back and forth over the same area as they search for mice and voles, before dropping down to grab their victim. They will often perch on fence posts and gates, particularly along roads, so can be seen from a bicycle or car. During the day they roost in farm buildings such as barns, where they can be easily disturbed.

Little Owl	
Average size	Length 21–23 cm, wingspan 54–58 cm, weight 140–220 gm
Behaviour	Crepuscular (seen at dawn or dusk) and diurnal
Range	Found in rural parts of lowland England and eastern and northern Wales, with a very few pairs in southern Scotland. Absent from towns, cities and upland areas, and not found in Ireland.
Breeding season	April to July
Eggs	3–4
Incubation period	29–31 days
Fledging period	37–40 days
Hunting habits	Hunts by dropping down onto its prey, often from the branch of a tree
Lifespan	Average 3 years
UK population	2,350 to 4,900 (average 3,600) pairs
European population	Between 560,000 and 1.3 million breeding pairs
How to find them	Little owls are the most diurnal of our three most common species of owl, and can often be seen during the daytime, perched on a branch of a tree, a fence or gatepost, or on top of a farm building. They are most active at the beginning or towards the end of the day.

Long-eared Owl	
Average size	Length 35–37 cm, wingspan 95 cm, weight 290 gm
Behaviour	Almost entirely nocturnal
Range	Breeds in woods and forests across much of central and eastern England, southern and eastern Scotland, and a few parts of Wales, western England and northern Scotland. The only species of owl that breeds in Ireland. In winter birds move further south.
Breeding season	March to July
Eggs	3–4
Incubation period	28 days
Fledging period	29–34 days
Hunting habits	Hunts unobtrusively in, around or on the edge of woods and forests, almost always by night
Lifespan	Average 4 years
UK population	1,800 to 6,000 (average 3,900) pairs
European population	Between 114,000 and 269,000 breeding pairs
How to find them	Long-eared owls are, like the tawny owl, birds of woodlands and, because of their almost entirely nocturnal habits, can be very hard to see. There is also a risk of disturbing them on their breeding territories, so searching for them at this time of year is not advisable. Your best chance is to visit a known winter roost, often on an official nature reserve, where the birds can be viewed during the daytime at a safe distance.

Short-eared Owl	
Average size	Length 37–39 cm, wingspan 102 cm, weight 330 gm
Behaviour	Diurnal
Range	In spring and summer, breeds on large areas of open moorland, mostly in upland areas of northern England, central Wales and Scotland, with highest numbers in the Western Isles and Orkney. In autumn and winter, short-eared owls head south to lowland grassland and wetland areas, often on the coast. Commoner in the east than the west of Britain, and absent from urban areas and the whole of Ireland.
Breeding season	April to July
Eggs	4–7
Incubation period	24–29 days
Fledging period	26–32 days
Hunting habits	Hunts low over moorlands in spring and summer, and farmland, marshes and coastal grasslands in autumn and winter
Lifespan	Average 3–4 years
UK population	620 to 2,000 (average 1,400) pairs
European population	Between 55,000 and 186,000 breeding pairs
How to find them	Short-eared owls are birds of the open countryside, preferring upland moors during the breeding season, and coastal marshes and rough grasslands for the rest of the year. Look out for a large, floppy-winged owl, appearing almost as big as a buzzard, as it covers large areas of habitat in search of voles and other prey. Occasionally seen perched on heather or on a fence post.

Snowy Owl	
Average size	Length 52–71 cm, wingspan 116–183 cm, weight 1.5–2.4 kg
Behaviour	Crepuscular; hunts by day, but usually more active at night
Range	A very rare visitor, with only a handful seen each year; mostly in the Scottish Highlands and Islands, but occasionally farther south, with a few records in East Anglia and the Isles of Scilly.
Breeding season	April to July
Eggs	5–11
Incubation period	32 days
Fledging period	18–25 days in nest; but still need parental care afterwards
Hunting habits	Ambushes prey by dropping down from perch or approaching in flight
Lifespan	Average 9 years
UK population	No regular breeding pairs
European population	Between 1,200 and 2,700 pairs
How to find them	Snowy owls are rare and irregular vagrants to Britain from the Arctic regions; you would be very lucky to find one. The best places to search are the high tops of the Cairngorms in the Scottish Highlands, and the Western Isles, including St Kilda. They can appear at any time of year, but are most likely in autumn and winter.

Eagle Owl	
Average size	Length up to 70 cm, wingspan 190 cm, weight 2.3–3.3 kg
Behaviour	Mostly nocturnal
Range	A very rare breeding bird, with an unknown number of birds (almost all escaped from captivity) at large in the wild; mostly in northern Britain.
Breeding season	March to July
Eggs	1–2 (occasionally 3–4)
Incubation period	31–36 days
Fledging period	35–49 days in nest
Hunting habits	Ambushes prey by dropping down from perch or approaching in flight
Lifespan	Average 9 years
UK population	No known regular breeding pairs, though there may be a number of escaped birds breeding in the wild
European population	Between 18,500 and 30,300 pairs
How to find them	Eagle owls are very rare in Britain, and any breeding sites are kept secret as they are at risk of being killed or the eggs stolen, so there are no public sites where you can watch these birds.

I

WHAT IS AN OWL?

Any bird of prey of the order Strigiformes . . . typically nocturnal and characterized by a large rounded head, raptorial beak, soft plumage, upright posture, and large eyes directed forwards and surrounded by a shallow cone of radiating feathers.

Oxford English Dictionary

The world's 10,800 or so species of bird – classified into roughly 250 different families – are wonderfully diverse. Yet the majority of birders, ornithologists, and indeed the general public, would surely agree that owls are, quite simply, unique.

Some other bird families, including the nightjars, nighthawks, frogmouths and potoos, are, like owls, largely nocturnal, while some species in other groups are also active after dark, such as parrots (kakapo and night parrot), waders (stone-curlew and the other thick-knees), seabirds (shearwaters and petrels), night herons, kiwis, and the nightingale. And, of course, many other species of bird frequently feed or sing under cover of darkness. But owls have adapted more radically than any other group of birds to a life lived mostly at night, and this is reflected in their appearance, morphology, habits and lifestyle.

Ancient writers placed owls alongside other predatory species that have hooked beaks and powerful claws, lumping them together as 'accipitres', or 'rapacious birds', and considering them to be closely related to diurnal raptors such as hawks and falcons. More recently, it was thought that they shared an evolutionary line with another predominately nocturnal family, nightjars. But as Mike Toms reveals in his comprehensive Collins New Naturalist volume *Owls*, the latest molecular analysis suggests that the apparent similarity of owls to nightjars is actually the result of convergent evolution: because both groups hunt at night, using similar techniques, they have developed superficial similarities in appearance.

This new scientific analysis places owls in the supergroup Coronaves, where they do indeed sit next to day-flying birds of prey: the order Accipitriformes, which includes hawks, eagles, kites, harriers and vultures (but not falcons, which are more closely related to parrots). So by linking owls with hawks, those early ornithologists were at least partly correct.

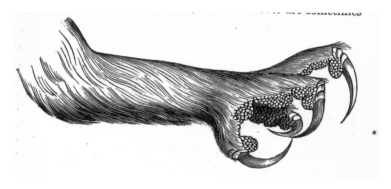

Nevertheless, being in their own separate order, Strigiformes, owls are sufficiently different to have their own unique and special features. They have a characteristically upright posture when perched, a large, broad head, extremely good hearing, powerful night vision and very soft, dense feathers that allow them to fly almost silently – and very slowly – when hunting their prey. As the eighteenth-century naturalist and vicar Gilbert White observed, 'Owls move in a buoyant manner, as if lighter than the air; they seem to want ballast.'

Other key features, which owls mostly share with other predators, include forward-facing eyes, giving them binocular vision; sharp talons, enabling them to seize and hold their prey without it escaping; and a sharp, down-curved, hooked bill. Typically, they are solitary (except when breeding) and mostly – though not always – nocturnal.

Unlike most diurnal raptors, however, owls often have a mottled, camouflaged plumage, mimicking both the colour and texture of their surroundings; this enables them to blend in very well with their background, and thus avoid being seen. That is even true of the most superficially obvious of owls, the snowy owl, whose bright white plumage, sometimes speckled with black, fits in surprisingly well with its typical surroundings of snow, and lichen-covered rocks and boulders.

If you are lucky enough to get a close-up view of an owl – perhaps at a daytime roost – you will notice that although overall the plumage is cryptic, some species have distinctive markings on their faces, brightly-coloured irises in their eyes (often yellow or orange) or, as with the long-eared and short-eared owls, distinctive ear tufts. All these features are used, especially by those birds that live in more open and less forested habitats such as moorland or grassland, to signal to one another at dawn or dusk.

They are, as noted by the nineteenth-century ornithologist Robert Mudie, author of *The Feathered Tribes of the British Isles*, surprisingly light, despite 'the apparent bulk of their bodies. An owl, in its plumage, looks a thick, stout, and even clumsy bird; but strip off the feathers, and it is really nothing.'

Mudie goes on to point out that 'The great owl *Strix bubo* [i.e. eagle owl], the size of which has been compared to that of the eagle, is not one-fourth of the weight.' Although this is an exaggeration – typically an eagle owl weighs about half as much as a golden eagle – his general point holds: owls are indeed much lighter than you might expect, as anyone who has ever had a captive barn owl perch on their wrist will know.

Although all owls are in the order Strigiformes, they have been subdivided into two different families: Strigidae (the true or typical owls), and Tytonidae (barn, masked and grass owls). The vast majority of species – well over 200 – are in the former group, with only about twenty in the latter, including our own familiar barn owl.

Owls are among the most widespread and adaptable of all the world's birds, found in all the world's geographical and ecological regions apart from a handful of remote, oceanic islands. Although mainly sedentary, roughly one in ten species are prone to wandering; indeed, a recent authoritative study, *Vagrancy in Birds* by Alexander Lees and James Gilroy, suggests that the difficulty in locating vagrant owls might be masking the true extent of their global travels.

As owls have, over time, spread around the world, they have managed to colonise a very wide variety of habitats, including dense tropical, temperate broad-leaved and northern boreal forests, grasslands and farmlands, coastal estuaries, freshwater marshes, Arctic tundra, islands and even the busy heart of our cities – I have occasionally heard tawny owls hooting even in the middle of London. In the process of successfully exploiting so many different habitats, they have adapted to survive and thrive in many different ways, although still remaining recognisably owls in their appearance, lifestyle and behaviour.

The world's two largest species of owl – Blakiston's fish owl and the marginally smaller Eurasian eagle owl – are huge and daunting predators: female Blakiston's fish owls can grow to 72 cm (28.3 inches) long, with a 180-cm (71-inch) wingspan, and weigh as much as 4.6 gm (over 10 lb). This is more than five times longer, and almost 150 times heavier, than the world's smallest species, the elf owl of North America, which at 13.5 cm (a shade over 5 inches), and weighing just 31 gm (barely more than one ounce), is actually smaller and lighter than the house sparrow. Two other very small species are the Tamaulipas pygmy owl, endemic to the mountain forests of north-eastern Mexico, and the long-whiskered owlet, which is restricted to a tiny area of the Andes cloud forests in northern Peru.

Large or small, one thing that unites owls, certainly compared with many other bird families, is their fairly uniform body shape and appearance – what scientists call their anatomy. One of their most characteristic features – although not easy to see unless you are looking at an owl's skeleton – is that they have a very broad skull, with a flat front.

This unique feature gives owls two major advantages: first, it allows room for large, round eyes that face more directly forward than those of other birds, including diurnal birds of prey. Second, the broad skull means that owls' ears are placed further apart than in other birds; so that sounds reach their ears at slightly different times.

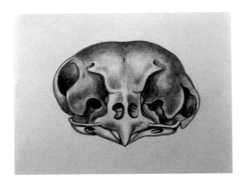

Unlike on other birds, their eyes are tubular rather than round, which, along with a higher proportion of light-sensitive rods, rather than colour-sensitive cones, gives them the ability to see well after dark. However, these adaptations also mean that owls are long-sighted, and so are unable to focus on close objects, and less good at distinguishing between colours.

In strong sunlight they can struggle to see at all, so they try to avoid being exposed to this whenever possible. As Gilbert White's contemporary, Thomas Bewick, observed, 'Unable to bear the brighter light of the sun, it retires to some lonely retreat, where it passes the day in silence and obscurity.'

When an owl is hunting – often under cover of darkness, when it is usually unable to use sight to find its prey – it will rely on its hearing. That is also often true during daylight hours, as many of the species targeted by a hunting owl, especially small mammals, do not normally show themselves, but instead hide away in long grass, dense leaves or heavy snow.

But using its ears to locate prey poses another problem: how will the owl hear the target over the sound of the air rushing through its wings? To reduce this extraneous noise to almost zero, owls have a series of small hooks and barbs on the edges of their flight feathers, which break up the air as it flows over the front edge of their wings, and channel it along their wings to the ends. This has the effect of reducing turbulence, and allows the birds to fly almost completely silently, as another early writer on birds, the Scottish ornithologist William MacGillivray, explained:

In accordance with the nocturnal habits of the Owls, a peculiarly noiseless and silent flight was necessary, to enable them to steal unawares upon a timid and vigilant [victim], and hover with ease while searching

1, Tawny Owl: Loosely constructed feather of juvenile plumage with one short filament of nestling down adhering near tip. 2, Barn-Owl: First winter feather with long 2nd nestling down adhering to its tip and two filaments of very short 1st nestling down adhering to tips of 2nd nestling down.

for a concealed or lurking prey . . . So gentle is the motion of their downy wings, that one is not by hearing rendered sensible of their immediate presence.

As well as this remarkable adaptation for silent flight, owls have developed another unique modification to their hearing. Some species, including the barn owls, as we have seen, and the Tengmalm's (also known as boreal) owl of northern Europe, have ears placed asymmetrically, one slightly higher than the other, to enable the bird to pinpoint the exact origin of a sound. This means that their skulls are lopsided.

These two species, along with others, including the Ural, great grey and saw-whet owls, have a very obvious, heart-shaped facial disk, which acts rather like a wildlife sound recordist's parabolic reflector, focusing and concentrating distant sounds into their ears. Try cupping your hands behind your ears when you listen to birdsong, and you'll appreciate the genuine improvement it brings in volume and clarity. This adaptation gives owls a real advantage when hunting, as it enables them to locate the rustle of a mouse or vole precisely. They also have a well-developed medulla, the part of the brain which enables a creature to aurally 'map' an area around itself, and in this further refine the owl's targeting of its prey.

Because a hunting owl hears the sound of its prey through its asymmetrical ears at slightly different times, it turns its head until the sounds arrive simultaneously, at which point it knows it is heading in the right direction. As the owl approaches its target, at the last moment it changes its body configuration, extending the talons out in front of its body, before striking quickly and efficiently to grab the unfortunate victim.

Once an owl has successfully caught its prey, it uses its short, curved bill, with that hooked tip and serrated edges, to tear apart its victim so it can feed. The bill is noticeably different in shape from that of diurnal raptors: instead of protruding in front of the bird, it faces downwards, and is closely tucked into the owl's face. When an owl is hunting, this gives it a clear field of vision, and avoids deflecting any incoming sound waves away from the facial disk.

Owls do, of course, use their eyesight, both for hunting, and to avoid predators – especially important for smaller species such as the little owl of Britain and Europe and the elf owl of North America. But this is where their front-facing eyes put them at a slight disadvantage, as they are unable to swivel them to look from side to side, as we can.

They have solved this problem by evolving the ability to rotate their necks and heads up to 270 degrees – three-quarters of an entire circle. They are able to do so because they have twice as many neck vertebrae as us – fourteen compared with just seven for humans – and other adaptations, which prevent the blood being cut off to their brain when they twist their head around.

Owls feed on a wide range of different prey, although for the majority of species the main items are small mammals, including rodents, such as rats, mice, voles and lemmings; lagomorphs (rabbits and hares);

and insectivores (shrews, moles and occasionally hedgehogs); while the larger species of owl may also take medium-sized mammals such as foxes.

In general, much of the mammalian prey on which owls feed comes under the category often termed 'vermin' or 'pests', which led the Victorian author (and Bishop of Norwich) Edward Stanley to commend them for their usefulness to mankind: 'We may say a more useful race of birds does not exist; since . . . their food consists entirely of vermin very prejudicial to our crops, and which, but for these nocturnal hunters, might do serious mischief.'

Most species of owl will take birds when they are available, the eagle owls even hunting down other avian predators such as buzzards, hawks and falcons. Smaller species, such as scops and screech owls, feed mostly on insects such as worms, moths and beetles; while others, including several Asian and African species, like Blakiston's fish owl of Japan and Pel's fishing owl of sub-Saharan Africa, specialise in hunting fish.

Even our own familiar tawny and barn owls will occasionally choose an aquatic diet: the Victorian explorer and early conservationist Charles Waterton was watching a barn owl hunting on a fine July evening, when 'all of a sudden she dropt perpendicularly into the water.' Thinking she had come to some harm, he continued to observe, and then 'I saw the owl rise out of the water with a fish in her claws, and take it to the nest.'

We know more about the diet of owls not just by observing them hunt – which can be tricky, given their mostly nocturnal habits – but also because, like many other birds, they regurgitate 'pellets'. These are spherical or oblong objects, a few centimetres in diameter, which contain all the material the owl has eaten but cannot digest, such as the fur, feathers, bones, claws and teeth from their victims. Typically, an owl will expel one pellet a couple of hours after each meal, and will not be able to feed again until it has done so.

Studying these pellets, usually by delicately pulling them apart and examining the contents with a magnifying glass, allows scientists to get a very clear idea of what a particular bird, or population of birds, is eating. With owls, pellets are fairly easy to find, often by searching beneath the trees or bushes where the birds roost. Looking at the contents can produce some unexpected surprises: for example, bird rings, which are accidentally consumed by any owls that regularly feed on avian prey.

Owls are not just hunters; they can also be hunted. Larger species like the eagle owls and fish owls have very few predators (apart, of course, from man) because of their size, and because they are at or near the top of the food chain. Nevertheless, European eagle owls have been predated by white-tailed and golden eagles, while in turn they will regularly hunt other, smaller species of owl.

All owls are vulnerable to being caught and killed by mammalian predators, especially when the female is on the nest, with chicks or eggs. Foxes, stoats and weasels, and almost any other opportunistic predator, will grab an easy meal if they can, as will snakes, especially in the tropics, and – if they get the chance – domestic dogs and cats.

Though owls are vulnerable to human interference, persecution and superstition, however, they are also widely celebrated, revered and loved, as the next chapter, 'Owls and Us', shows.

2

OWLS AND US

Now fades the glimmering landscape on the sight,
And all the air a solemn stillness holds . . .
Save that from yonder ivy-mantled tower,
The moping owl does to the moon complain
Of such as, wandering near her secret bower,
Molest her ancient solitary reign.

Thomas Gray, 'Elegy Written in a Country
Churchyard' (1751)

'The very name', wrote ornithologist Robert Mudie in 1834, 'is a name of lamentation, expressive of the sound of its note, which is one of the most melancholy love-songs in the whole chorus of nature. Superstition has accordingly laid hold of the bird, as one of the instruments with which to bind the ignorant in fetters of fear.'

Like so many other English bird names, 'owl' is onomatopoeic, based on the bird's sound. It derives from Germanic languages, going back to at least before the birth of Christ, and almost certainly much further. Its first written appearance in what is recognisably English – spelt phonetically, as 'hule' – dates back to around AD 1250 (perhaps even earlier), in the title of the medieval poem 'The Owl and the Nightingale'.

The sense of owls as primeval beings from an unimaginably past time is captured in the lines quoted at the start of this chapter, from one of the best-known and best-loved poems in the English language, Thomas Gray's mid-eighteenth-century 'Elegy Written in a Country Churchyard', as the unnamed human intruder disturbs the owl's 'ancient solitary reign'. This shadowy, spectral aura is reinforced, as Robert Mudie noted in an evocative passage, by the nature of the places where owls live:

Deep shady groves, hollow-trees, crumbling ruins clad with ivy, steeples and churches with their associations of graves and ghosts – all that seems dim to the reason of man, all that stands monumental of the works of nature . . . The owls, in these places – often heard, but seldom seen: when heard, heard in the gloom and the stillness of the night; and when seen, appearing with something of judge-like solemnity – made them very readily convertible into a sort of 'doom-birds'.

But this association with superstition and portent, which runs through our culture and literature from the earliest times, is not confined to the past. Owls remain at the centre of modern myths, legends, stories, poems, songs and popular culture, wherever in the world we look. As I suggested in the Prologue, this is largely down to their mostly nocturnal nature, the very antithesis of our own diurnal lifestyle, but also, perhaps, because our encounters with their world tend to be transitory and indeterminate.

Much like other birds central to our folklore, such as the raven, our conception of owls' meaning and significance is very fluid – and often utterly contradictory. They can be cute and cuddly, or cruel and vicious; good, or evil; bringers of wisdom, or messengers of doom, death and destruction. Owls can be all things to all people: a template onto which we project our own feelings and beliefs.

The darker side of owl mythology features prominently in *Metamorphoses*, a narrative poem written in Latin by the Roman poet Ovid, dating back over 2,000 years to about the time of the birth of Christ. In one memorable episode, the goddess Persephone, having been abducted and forced to remain as queen of the underworld for half the year, flies into a rage when given a message confirming her fate by Ascalaphus. In a classic case of 'blaming the messenger', she turns the unfortunate man into an owl – a bird of ill-omen, as in this evocative translation from the Greek by the first Poet Laureate, John Dryden:

> But now a queen, she with resentment heard,
> And chang'd the vile informer to a bird.
> In Phlegeton's black stream her hand she dips,
> Sprinkles his head, and wets his babling lips.
> Soon on his face, bedropt with magick dew,
> A change appear'd, and gawdy feathers grew.
> A crooked beak the place of nose supplies,
> Rounder his head, and larger are his eyes.
> His arms and body waste, but are supply'd
> With yellow pinions flagging on each side.
> His nails grow crooked, and are turn'd to claws,
> And lazily along his heavy wings he draws.
> Ill-omen'd in his form, the unlucky fowl,
> Abhorr'd by men, and call'd a schrieching owl.

The Romans believed that if an owl were nailed to a door, this would avert evil; yet they simultaneously thought that witches could turn into owls and suck the blood of babies. The deaths of key Romans, including Julius Caesar, Augustus and Agrippa, were supposedly foretold by the unexpected appearance of owls during the daytime. In the opening Act of Shakespeare's *Julius Caesar*, the owl is 'the bird of night', an augurer, which

> yesterday, did sit
> Even at noon-day, upon the marketplace,
> Hooting and shrieking.

Another story tells of how the unexpected appearance of owls during the daytime in Rome portended the Romans' impending defeat by the Parthians at Carrhae, on the plains of the Rivers Tigris and Euphrates in present-day Turkey. The generals failed to heed the birds' warning and, despite a huge superiority of numbers, their army was soundly beaten. With as many as 20,000 men killed and a further 10,000 taken prisoner, this was one of the most humiliating defeats in the history of the Roman Empire.

A wide range of owls, most notably the 'horned owl', which we now call the eagle owl, are condemned by Pliny the Elder, the first century AD Roman writer and naturalist, in his masterwork *Natural History*, for their malign portent:

> The horned owl is especially funereal, and is greatly abhorred in all auspices of a public nature: it inhabits deserted places, and not only desolate spots, but those of a frightful and inaccessible nature: the monster of the night, its voice is heard, not with any tuneful note, but emitting a sort of shriek. Hence it is that it is looked upon as a direful omen to see it in a city, or even so much as in the day-time.

In the same work, however, he apparently recommends two raw owls' eggs (or alternatively a decapitated, and then fried, canary) as a hangover cure!

Several centuries earlier than Pliny and Ovid, the Ancient Greeks had a rather more positive attitude towards owls; especially the little owl, which was closely associated with the goddess Athene. As well as the terracotta vase featuring Athene looking at a hovering little owl I discuss in Chapter 5, another precious vase, dating back to *c.* 500 BC, features the bird as its principal image, alongside an inscription reading 'ΔΕΜΟΣΙΟΣ' – in modern script, DEMOSIOS – meaning 'belonging to the people'. Such depictions of the little owl in Ancient Greek culture appear to be the start of that long and enduring link between owls and wisdom.

Between the Greek and Roman eras, the Old Testament of the Bible, composed from roughly 1500 BC to 400 BC, frequently mentions owls – almost always negatively. Under Judaism's Mosaic Law they were regarded, along with other birds of prey and scavengers such as crows, ravens and vultures, as 'unclean', as this remarkably comprehensive list from the Book of Leviticus shows:

> These are the birds you are to regard as unclean and not eat because they are unclean: the eagle, the vulture, the black vulture, the red kite, any kind of black kite, any kind of raven, the horned owl, the screech owl, the gull, any kind of hawk, the little owl, the cormorant, the great owl, the white owl, the desert owl, the osprey, the stork, any kind of heron, the hoopoe and the bat.

An apocalyptic – and again superbly detailed – passage from Isaiah illustrates how owls can come to symbolise mourning, loneliness, and also the desolation consequent on divine retribution, as it warns of the vengeance of the Lord on the land:

> The desert owl and screech owl will possess it; the great owl and the raven will nest there . . . Thorns will overrun her citadels, nettles and brambles her strongholds. She will become a haunt for jackals, a home for owls.

Other societies cast owls in different roles. Native Americans saw owls as guardians of knowledge, and also as messengers between this world and the afterlife. They were regarded as soothsayers, able to

predict cold weather; something likely to have a basis in truth. When the great grey owl was out hunting, freezing weather was thought to be imminent, meaning that the fire should be stoked and more wood gathered. But the sound of an owl might also be a sign that the spirits were calling you. If you answered the call of a boreal owl with a whistle, but the owl failed to call back, death would soon follow. Even dreaming about an owl was bad news – again, signifying imminent death. The Cheyenne tribe, however, regarded owls as the protective spirits of the night, and would wear their feathers in battle to give them, it was believed, the ability to move silently at night and see in the dark.

Owls often feature in the folklore of other ancient cultures as emissaries from other worlds. For the Aztecs of Mexico, and the Hindus of India, they brought messages from beyond the grave, while the Aborigines of Australia connected them with a bogeyman who seized and ate children.

Across much of the world – including Britain and Europe – people have long regarded owls as being connected with sorcery and evil, and harbingers of death. The cultural historian Boria Sax notes that owls might represent the dangers of the unknown – woods and forests – historically regarded as 'the domain of sorcerers and dangerous beasts', as opposed to the relative security of the village. This idea can be found in many European fairy tales, in which the mysterious forest surrounding human habitations is the home of scary and potentially lethal creatures, such as the wolf in 'Little Red Riding Hood'.

Unfortunately, in some parts of sub-Saharan Africa, those beliefs have led to the birds being widely persecuted and killed for food, medicine and witchcraft – indeed, they still do, as a scholarly and detailed study reveals. 'Owls Used as Food and Medicine and for Witchcraft in Africa' was published in 2022 by the world's leading owl expert, Finnish ornithologist Heimo Mikkola.

Between 1996 and 2002, Dr Mikkola and his colleagues carried out extensive face-to-face interviews in twenty different African countries, speaking to people responsible for hundreds of owl killings.[1] Acutely sensitive to being accused of cultural appropriation or post-colonial attitudes, Mikkola (who lived in six different African countries for more than two decades, and worked in over thirty more) co-operated closely with cultural experts from the regions involved, who conducted in-depth, face-to-face interviews using a questionnaire translated into a wide range of regional languages.

The findings were fascinating, if rather depressing: in roughly one in six cases, the birds were killed because they were seen as an ill omen, likely to bring death or disaster. In another one in six cases, they were

---

[1] These included countries in East Africa (Botswana, Kenya, Tanzania and Uganda); Southern Africa (Lesotho, Mozambique, Zambia, Zimbabwe, Malawi, Namibia and South Africa); and West Africa (Angola, Cameroon, Ghana, Guinea, Liberia, Nigeria, Senegal, Sierra Leone and the Gambia).

killed for food, although in Sierra Leone, where food shortages are more common, that figure rose to almost half. A smaller proportion – about 6 per cent – were used in traditional medicine, and a further 28 per cent for magic and witchcraft; including the belief that sacrificing an owl would result in the death of another human being.

Mikkola points out that the victims were simply seen as 'owls', with no distinction being made between rare and endangered, as opposed to common and widespread. As a result, the victims included several very rare species, including the critically endangered Anjouan and Mohéli scops owls (both endemic to the Comoro Islands, between Mozambique and Madagascar), and the rufous fishing owl of West Africa.

Persecution of owls – for a wide range of cultural and practical reasons – is far from confined to these regions. As already noted, Judaism has long considered owls – along with other raptors – as 'unclean', while farmers in Europe and North America have in the past often killed owls, even though these help reduce the numbers of rodents in their barns. According to Mark Cocker, in parts of France and Switzerland, as recently as the 1960s, barn owls were regularly nailed to the doors of farm buildings to ward off evil.

Back in Britain, similar fears are harboured: the barn owl leads the way in folklore and superstition – indeed, wherever they are found around the world, barn owls play their part in tales of horror, ghosts and spirits: a recent survey of 300 people in the UK found that almost two in five considered owls to be 'scary'.

A barn owl might also be the explanation behind a curious and rather chilling modern tale, of the Cornish 'Owlman'. The story begins on an April day in 1976, when two young sisters were playing in the churchyard at Mawnan, just south of Falmouth, while their mother and father prepared a picnic nearby. A few minutes later, the girls returned to their parents, terrified at what they claimed to have seen: a large, bird-like human, with long, rounded wings, hovering menacingly over the church tower.

An account of this strange phenomenon, together with a drawing the family had made, was later published in the paranormal publication the *Fortean Times*, following which – surprise, surprise – more sightings were reported. If we discount the possibility that these were some kind of spoof made by a local wanting to scare visitors to the churchyard (unlikely, given that there were only a handful of reports over twenty years), it seems most likely that what the witnesses actually saw was simply a barn owl, emerging unexpectedly from its daytime roost.

The notion that the Owlman is an urban (or in this case, rural) myth gains credence from a video taken in 2017, in the city of Visakhapatnam, in India's Andhra Pradesh. The video, which soon went viral on social media, appears to show two extra-terrestrial aliens, with thin, white bodies, standing bolt upright, while staring back at the camera with empty black eye sockets. In fact, the 'aliens' were baby barn owls, about two or three weeks old, which, having been startled by a human intruder, had risen up onto their feet and were rocking nervously from side to side.

The 'aliens' and Owlman mysteries aside, we might assume that these mostly ancient – and to be honest often rather bizarre – beliefs have no place in modern culture and society. Yet the popularity of owls, regarded in both positive and negative ways, does not appear to be fading. Of modern incarnations, the most famous is Hedwig the snowy owl, in the Harry Potter books and films (see Chapter 7).

Countless other children's stories feature a (usually comforting) owl character, such as 'Wol' in A. A. Milne's Winnie-the-Pooh books, and Edward Lear's nonsense verse 'The Owl and the Pussycat', while Pablo Picasso, Florence Nightingale and Theodore Roosevelt all kept pet owls. The Oscar-nominated actor Salma Hayek even gave a pet scops owl to her husband, François-Henri Pinault – after all, what else can you give a billionaire?

Sometimes the fascination with owls is positively educational: the wildlife artist Robert Fuller, based in the Yorkshire Wolds, has more than 100 hidden cameras broadcasting live feeds on the Internet. Of these, the most popular are his local barn, tawny and little owls: one brief video clip of a young barn owl reacting to the sound of thunder has had 24 million views and almost one million 'likes'.

Other representations of owls in western societies are, unfortunately, more commercialised, cheap and tacky. Typical owl trinketry is the unidentifiable, identikit version with large eyes and a cute appearance used to flog jewellery, plant pots, toys, pillows, garden ornaments, clothing, arts and crafts, and much else. Owl merchandising has a long pedigree: in December 2022, Spanish scientists revealed that the very first mass-produced children's toy was not some post-war product, nor even a Victorian curiosity; it was a piece of slate-carved sand decorated in the recognisable shape and image of an owl, found in a tomb that was more than 5,000 years old.

The main reason why we are so fascinated by owls surely comes down to their appearance: very few animals, apart from primates such as orang-utans, gorillas and chimpanzees, and perhaps dolphins, have a 'face', like us. The owl's huge eyes, and the large, rounded head, are almost a Disney caricature of what we imagine a cute creature should look like.

In which case, why have owls consistently triggered the very opposite effect in us: unease – even terror? Here the concept of the 'uncanny valley', formulated in 1970 by a Japanese robotics professor, Masahiro Mori, may be pertinent. This seeks to explain why human likeness in something that is not human prompts in us not the apparently logical emotional response of kinship and affinity, but more often a rather creepy feeling. Paradoxically, given that we react most negatively to wild creatures that look *least* like us (snakes, scorpions and spiders, for example), when something looks *rather* like a human being, but not quite, we still tend to respond negatively. This may be because, although we react favourably to the 'human' aspect of an owl's appearance, when the bird then refuses to engage with us we feel somehow snubbed, which engenders hostility.

Interestingly, some eminent ornithologists have not always been convinced by the beauty, charisma and fascination of owls, as the Victorian naturalist William Yarrell admitted:

> The characters and appearance of Owls are so singular and so peculiar, that once having seen them they are not readily forgotten. They have but little external beauty of form. The head is large, the expression grotesque, the body bulky in appearance, the plumage soft and downy.

Either way, as Jeremy Mynott observes in *Birdscapes*, owls 'present themselves to us with more associations than perhaps any other family of birds'. From Palaeolithic cave paintings to Pokémon characters, owls have always fascinated, captivated and terrified us, depending on the time, place and context. In the following chapters, I will delve into the lives, habits, behaviour and cultural connections of Britain's seven species of owl – the tawny, barn, little, short-eared and long-eared, snowy, and eagle owls – before a final chapter on the world's other species of owls, and my encounters with some of them during my global travels.

A.Thorburn

$\frac{1}{3}$

Litho. W. Greve, Berlin.

3

TAWNY OWL

Then nightly sings the staring owl,
Tu-whit; Tu-who – a merry note . . .

William Shakespeare, *Love's Labour's Lost,*
Act V, Scene II (1597)

The tawny owl is, even more than other owls, something of a paradox. It is by far the commonest species of owl in Britain, with an estimated 50,000 breeding pairs – about the same as the far more visible Canada goose – yet we hardly ever see it, because of its almost entirely nocturnal lifestyle.

Rarely seen, maybe, but often heard: the tawny owl's famous *tu-whit, tu-whoo* call is one of the best-known and most distinctive of all our bird sounds. Yet even this is a misperception. Shakespeare was wrong when he attributed the familiar call to a single bird: the sound is actually a rare example of an avian duet. It is the male that utters the hooting *tu-whoo*, while the female responds, in the gaps between his hoots, with a high-pitched *tu-whit* – often rendered as *kee-wick*, with the stress on the second syllable.

William MacGillivray, who in his rather pedantic way wanted to change the species name to 'Tawny Hooting-owl', described the sound as 'a loud and doleful cry'. The poet John Clare (1793–1864) agreed:

Shaksper [*sic*] calls it a 'merry note'. Tis hard to call his taste into question but I really must confess my ignorance that I cannot find a reason why he makes it so. It sounds in my ear always as it did in Grays [Thomas Gray's 'Elegy'] a note that bespoke complaining sadness rather than merriment.

MacGillivray quoted the eighteenth-century French ornithologist Georges-Louis Leclerc, Comte de Buffon, who noted that the call 'has a considerable resemblance to the cry of the wolf, a circumstance which induced the Latins to give it the name *Ulula*, which comes from *ululare*, to howl or cry like the wolf'. Buffon's contemporary, Gilbert White, observed that 'when brown owls hoot their throats swell as big as a hen's egg,' and that their call sounds very much like a human voice – hence our ability to imitate it, perhaps.

Sometimes, however, this can lead to misunderstandings. A few years ago, one of the tabloid newspapers reported that two women were chatting to one another while waiting for the washing to dry in their local launderette, when one casually mentioned that her husband went out every evening to look for a tawny owl, which he attempted to attract by imitating its hooting call. 'That's funny,' replied her companion, 'my husband does exactly the same thing.' It was only then that they both realised, to their great amusement, that the hooting sound of the 'owl' that each man could hear was, in fact, being produced by their fellow bird enthusiast.

From late autumn onwards, through the long nights of winter, and all the way into early spring, I regularly hear both male and female tawny owls genuinely calling from my wooded Somerset garden. This is usually by night, but occasionally, for reasons I shall explain later, during the day. The hooting of the male tawny was also the very first owl call I ever heard, at the age of seven or eight, from my bedroom in the London suburbs.

Since then I have listened to their unmistakable sound, at once comforting and strangely spooky, in places as diverse as west London's Ladbroke Square, the heart of the Caledonian pine forests of the Scottish Highlands, and on evening woodland walks all over Britain.

If you do manage to get a glimpse of a tawny (or as it used to be known, brown) owl, it looks exactly like the kind of owl a child might draw. It has a large, rounded head, round eyes that face forward, as if the bird is gazing back at you, and a rich, chestnut-brown plumage mottled with light and dark streaks, which helps it stay camouflaged in its woodland home. Some birds show a much greyer hue to their plumage, a variation that is commoner in mainland Europe than in Britain, but which I have occasionally come across here.

The tawny is the largest and heaviest of our common species of owl (though much smaller and lighter than the very rare snowy and eagle owls). Females are usually slightly longer, and noticeably heavier, than their mates.

Like many native British birds, the tawny owl evolved to live in the vast areas of dense forest and more open woodland pasture that once would have blanketed much of our landscape. Today, tawny owls continue to breed in wooded habitats across much of lowland Britain, though are absent from Scotland's Northern and Western Isles, and from the Isle of Man and Ireland. Globally, the species can be found across much of Europe and Asia, from Portugal in the west to the Indian sub-continent in the east. The world population is estimated to number between one million and three million individuals, of which at least a third, and probably more, are in Europe.

Until very recently, the tawny owl had not been recorded at all in Ireland, no doubt because of its reluctance to cross large expanses of open water. Records from the late nineteenth century turned out to be birds that had escaped from private collections; but in May 2013, a tawny owl was photographed during daylight hours at a National Trust estate in County Down, where it was being noisily pestered by various songbirds. As the photographer Craig Nash recalled,

> I heard it almost immediately I got there and tried to find the exact tree it was calling from. I was helped by three blackbirds, a mistle thrush and a song thrush, all who were mobbing the bird deep in some bushes. I still couldn't see it when, all of a sudden, I looked at my level rather than in the tree tops and – bingo – there it was, one beautiful tawny owl.

At first, observers thought the bird might also be an escapee from a captive collection but, with none reported missing, they decided it must have crossed over from Great Britain during easterly storms earlier that spring. Once the news got out, attracting many birders and other curious visitors, it turned out that the estate staff had heard the owl hooting for some time, and it had probably been present for at least a month before it was officially discovered.

Back on the British mainland, tawny owls are fairly adaptable. Although they are most likely to be found in large areas of mixed or deciduous woodland, they also breed in conifer plantations, large suburban and rural gardens, and even in urban parks, including those in central London.

In Andrew Self's *The Birds of London*, the tawny owl is described as 'a common resident and widespread breeder', with the first record, at Vauxhall in 1778, reported by none other than Gilbert White, on a rare visit to town from his rural Hampshire home. During the late 1950s, tawny owls could be found in no fewer than fourteen separate locations in inner London, including several leafy squares, and although they have since declined in the city centre, they are still breeding in many locations in and around the capital.

Of all our owls, the tawny is by far the most sedentary, with breeding pairs staying put on their territories all year round and, during the whole of their lifetime, rarely travelling more than a few kilometres from where they were born. They have a very small hunting territory: covering just 12–20 hectares (30–50 acres), about the same area as fifteen to twenty-five football pitches. This is far smaller than the territory of the barn owl, which in winter can cover up to 5,000 hectares: between 250 and over 400 times the size of the tawny's home range. Having a very small territory helps tawny owls familiarise themselves with the best places to hunt their rodent prey under cover of darkness.

It also means, as the medievalist and writer Michael J. Warren has noted in an article and his forthcoming book, *The Cuckoo's Lea*, that a number of English place names commemorate the ubiquitous presence of tawny owls: 'Earlier this year my family moved house to an estate just off Ulcombe Road, leading to the tiny village of Ulcombe nestled in a gentle fold of the North Downs.' As he goes on to explain, the name of this village, near Maidstone in the heart of Kent, derives from 'owl combe', meaning 'owl's valley'. Mentioned in the eleventh-century *Domesday Book*, the name is almost certainly much older than this: as Warren notes, 'ule' goes all the way back to Indo-European, several millennia before the birth of Christ, and must surely be an onomatopoeic representation of the call of the male tawny owl.

This is confirmed by the doyen of ornithological linguists, Professor

W. B. Lockwood, who traces the origin of the word back to prehistoric times. Other place names derived from the tawny owl's call include Oldcoates in Nottinghamshire and Outchester, Ulgham and Howltham in Northumberland. But beware, other places that appear to be named after owls, such as Uldale in Cumbria, actually derive from an Old Norse word for wolf, 'ulfa'.

Warren goes on to suggest that 'the onomatopoeic potency' of the word 'ule' in these owl-based place names means that our ancestors identified and perceived those places as soundscapes as much as landscapes, 'imagined and responded to through sonic texture and colour'. Once again, our primary connection with these birds of the night is through their sounds.

The tawny owl's sedentary nature and small, localised territory have led, each autumn, to an annual battle between established breeding pairs and their newly-adult offspring. By then, the young birds have become independent, and are trying to establish their own territory, which often brings them into direct conflict with their parents. So, from early autumn through to late winter, the adult males become more vocal, as they seek to 'kick out the teenagers' and maintain their own, solitary presence.

A few years ago, I heard a male tawny owl hooting persistently from just outside my office window. Nothing very unusual about that, you might think – except that this was not during the night, but at eleven o'clock in the morning, on a bright, late autumn day. At first, I assumed the sound was being made by a fellow birder, playing a practical joke on me. But when I heard it again the following morning, I realised that this really was a male tawny owl hooting in broad daylight. Since then, I have heard tawny owls call during the day at other times of the year, including sunny afternoons in spring and summer, suggesting that this is more common behaviour than I had first thought.

Once the youngsters have finally been driven away – though not usually very far – their parents get down to the serious business of breeding. Tawny owls generally use a hole in a tree, but sometimes make an open nest on a rock or cliff face, or even on the ground. John Clare recalls a memorable confrontation with a tawny owl when, as a curious child, he attempted to steal its eggs:

> There was an old tree in a thicket . . . which had an owl's nest in it yearly. In one of my attempts to rob it the owl attacked me in so fierce a manner that I believed it to be no other than a witch in the shape of an owl and I fell from the tree and never after attempted to rob it again.

Tawnies are very early nesters, occasionally laying their clutch of two or three rounded, white eggs by February, though usually some time during March or April. Like most other species of owl, the female will begin to incubate soon after the first egg has been laid, meaning that the young hatch at different times, each after roughly a month.

If there is plenty of food available, all the chicks will survive to fledging, between five and six weeks later; if there are food shortages, then this strategy maximises the chances of at least the eldest one reaching

adulthood. Young tawny owls are looked after by their parents for a very long time; as long as six months. Even so, they are very vulnerable once they become independent in late autumn, and have less than a one in three chance of surviving to their first birthday.

If they do manage to get that far, they may live to about four years old, although the British record saw a ringed wild bird survive to the incredible age of almost twenty-three years and six months. The main causes of death for both young and adult tawny owls are collisions with electricity pylons, overhead wires, cars and other road vehicles, and also a shortage of food, especially during prolonged periods of wet weather.

When the youngsters do leave the nest, they have not yet fledged into their adult plumage. Instead, still sporting their dirty-white and fluffy juvenile plumage, they shuffle out and perch on a tree branch near their nest hole, in a behaviour known as 'branching'.

A quarter of a century ago, I was filming the very first episode of the TV series *Birding with Bill Oddie* at the RSPB's Minsmere reserve on the Suffolk coast, when we came upon something remarkable. 'Three baby tawny owls,' exclaimed Bill, 'looking like a bunch of feather dusters . . . It's not a rare bird but it is a rare sight, giving us an unforgettable experience.' That in a lifetime's birding Bill had never seen this before – and neither had I – shows just how elusive baby tawny owls can be.

The only other way to see tawny owls, outside the hours of night-time, is to discover one at its daytime roost: usually in the fork, or sometimes inside a hole or cavity, of a large, mature tree. The best way to do this is to listen carefully to the other woodland or parkland birds: usually blackbirds, thrushes, tits and finches, which 'mob' the owl, while uttering a series of loud and angry calls, to try to drive it away. 'That small birds . . . have a great dislike to owls is clear,' the nineteenth-century writer Edward Stanley observed, 'from the uproar that takes place if an unfortunate Owl is disturbed in the daytime . . . pursued, as

it is sure to be, by a host of them, who persecute it by every means in their power.'

Thomas Bewick noted that if tawny owls are disturbed at their daytime roost, 'they will utter an inward tremulous hooting of too-whoo, the subdued and gloomy shivering of which is peculiarly horrific.' An 'owl by day', writes Shakespeare in *Henry VI Part 3*, is to 'be mock'd and wonder'd at'.

A few years ago, on a sunny spring afternoon, I was taking a party of visiting birders for a walk along Hodder's Combe in Somerset's Quantock Hills, when we heard an unusual volley of songbird calls from the trees alongside the path. Sure enough, a quick scan with the binoculars revealed a flustered tawny owl, suffering a noisy onslaught from these much smaller and very brave birds. Eventually, and reluctantly, it flew off, still pursued by those angry sounds.

Perhaps they were not in too much danger. As the early nineteenth-century ornithologist George Montagu pointed out of the tawny owl, 'The light is very offensive to it, and in the sun it can scarcely see at all; so defective is it of sight in a bright day.'

Yet sometimes tawny owls do get their own back: in *London Birds* (1949), Richard Fitter tells of how the mid-twentieth-century nature writer Henry Williamson (of *Tarka the Otter* fame) 'knew a London tawny owl that used to creep under the trees where birds roosted and climb up to catch them; once he saw it seize in its talons a sparrow that had been mobbing it.' 'Williamson seems to have had more luck than anyone else in seeing London owls at the kill,' muses Fitter: 'he has watched a little owl pounce on a sparrow in Trafalgar Square, and a barn owl pounce in the gardens of the Temple.'

Like those species, tawny owls do occasionally hunt during daylight hours (and not just at dawn and dusk); especially during harsh winter weather, when food might be scarce. In his superb monograph *The*

Tawny Owl, Jeff R. Martin notes that the first report of daytime hunting in tawny owls comes from just over a century ago when, in a note in *British Birds*, E. U. Savage reported one taking a red squirrel near Carlisle. This has never been common or frequent behaviour, but might sometimes reflect new opportunities for the owls: for example, they have recently been seen in London's Kensington Gardens, hunting the introduced – and now abundant – rose-ringed (ring-necked) parakeets.

Along with most birds of prey, whether diurnal or nocturnal, the tawny owl mainly specialises in feeding on a particular group: in its case, small mammals such as mice, voles and shrews. But like most predators, it is adaptable and opportunistic in its hunting habits. Given the chance, tawny owls will catch and eat small birds, bats, frogs, earthworms and beetles, and virtually anything else within reach. 'The young of the brown owl will eat indiscriminately all that is brought,' wrote Gilbert White: 'snails, rats, kittens, puppies, magpies, and any kind of carrion or offal.'

During the 2014 series of the popular BBC natural history show *Springwatch* (also broadcast from Minsmere), the more unusual prey items brought back to the nest included a treecreeper, several slugs, a slow worm and a young moorhen. Many of these would have been obtained by the classic 'sit-and-wait' method of hunting, in which the owl perches unobtrusively on the branch of a tree, before dropping down silently to seize its unwary victim. Like other raptors that mainly hunt in woodlands, such as the sparrowhawk, tawny owls have shortish, rounded wings, which enable them to fly through their wooded habitat, and avoid obstacles more easily, than if they had longer ones.

They will occasionally hunt in flight, or by landing on the ground and searching the area around them for invertebrates such as worms. John F. Burton, formerly head of the BBC Natural History Unit's sound library, recalls that when he was a young man in the late 1940s, he found the remains of a number of large beetles on the ground in London's

Greenwich Park. He suspected that they had been dug up from the surrounding area, as they were immediately beneath a tawny owl's favourite roosting tree.

They will also scavenge for food, and have occasionally been observed feeding on dead rabbits by the side of a country road. Sometimes they take fish – either exotic species such as goldfish from garden ponds, or native ones from lakes and streams, as William Yarrell noted: 'Several writers have proved that this Owl feeds occasionally on fish, and that it is able to catch either those species that swim near the surface in deep water, or the bullhead and loach, that are to be found among stones in the shallowest parts of brooks.' Edward Stanley confirmed this, but went on (as he tended to do) to draw false and unfounded conclusions: 'It has been conjectured by some, that as fish are attracted by a light or any shining substance, there may be a luminous appearance in the large, round, and bright eyes of an Owl ... by which the fish are attracted within reach of its beak or claws.'

If tawny owls find an easy concentration of potential prey, they will return again and again to feed. In his 1900 book *Our Rarer British*

Breeding Birds, the pioneering bird photographer Richard Kearton told the story of a gamekeeper who could not work out what could be taking his young pheasants, as he had already destroyed all the vermin nearby: 'One dull evening, while sitting near his coops, gun athwart on his knees and briar [pipe] in course of being filled, he saw a tawny owl sail noiselessly out of an adjoining wood, snatch up one of his young pheasants, and fly off with it.' The keeper reacted just in time to shoot the owl dead. When he picked up the corpse, the young pheasant was still locked in its talons. Amazingly, when he released the tiny creature, it ran straight back to its mother, 'apparently none the worse for its strange experience'.

Although never popular with gamekeepers, tawny owls are, like most members of their family, much loved by the general public. They frequently appear on greetings cards, on the covers of children's books, and on a series of notebooks mainly aimed at teenage children, with titles like, 'I Just Really Like Tawny Owls, OK?', 'Just a Girl Who Loves a Tawny Owl', and even 'It's a Tawny Owl Thing, You Wouldn't Understand.' All these titles, and their accompanying child-like designs, stress the supposed 'cuteness' of the species: its round face and large, staring eyes. Yet the tawny owl is, above all else, a superb predator and, apart from its nocturnal habits, no different from diurnal raptors such as eagles, hawks, kites and falcons, which tend to be far less popular among the general public.

A few years after we moved to Somerset, my young daughter Daisy ran into the house one day, full of excitement. 'There's a hawk in the greenhouse!' she exclaimed. And there was: a young male sparrow-hawk, which had mistakenly flown through the open door and then, fortunately, managed to slow down and stop before it crashed into the glass at the far end. As I gingerly extracted the bird, it stared at me with those piercing yellow eyes, in a way that made me imagine the last moments of a small bird facing annihilation.

The next day, we had another encounter with a predator. This time it was my wife Suzanne who, while walking to the village shop, came across a dead tawny owl by the side of the road – presumably hit by a passing car. She brought it home, and we all gathered round to marvel at its soft plumage, and what can only be described as that kindly facial expression.

When I mentioned these two encounters to my friends and colleagues, the response was always the same: along the lines of, 'What a pity the owl was killed . . .' I wondered how they would have reacted if the owl had been rescued alive, and the sparrowhawk found dead. I somehow knew that their sympathy would have remained with the owl.

A few years later, I worked on the 'red button' interactive element of *Springwatch* at Minsmere. One of the highlights – not just for me, but for the audience watching at home – was the camera showing a sparrow-hawk's nest. This allowed us to observe, live and in real time, the chicks hatching out of the eggs, followed by the busy male returning regularly with food for his mate and her young.

After the series had ended, and we had returned home, we heard the news that a tawny owl nesting nearby had raided the sparrowhawk nest

and seized and killed the chicks. While this is, of course, perfectly natural behaviour, we still felt rather sad. But I wondered, once again, what our reaction would have been had the sparrowhawk killed the baby owls, instead of the other way round.

Tawny owls are not only aggressive towards their intended prey; they can also be hostile towards any human beings who deliberately or inadvertently enter their home territory, by night or day. Henry

Williamson – who certainly seems to have had a special affinity with owls as well as otters – was walking through London's Hyde Park one day when he was ambushed by a day-flying owl. The bird struck him hard on his head with its sharp talons, knocking his hat clean off. This turned out to be a female, whose nest was in the hollow of a branch above him, and of which he was completely unaware until she struck.

Attacks by tawny owls on humans are rare, but still occasionally occur, with a number of verified reports over the years. In April 2003, as Jeff Martin relates, a birder walking through a woodland in north Devon heard a strange clicking sound. As he turned to see what it was, he was struck on the head by a tawny owl, causing wounds to his head and ear.

Anyone familiar with the history of bird photography in Britain, meanwhile – and in particular the life of the acknowledged pioneer of the craft, Eric Hosking – will know that this man had an especially lucky escape. Today, Hosking is widely celebrated as, arguably, the world's best-known bird photographer; indeed, he has been described as 'the man who practically invented wildlife photography'. Born in London in 1909, and hooked on photography since he had been given a five-shilling Kodak Box Brownie at the age of seven or eight, he left school at fifteen with few qualifications, and a harsh verdict from his headmaster: 'Hosking, you'll never make anything of your life.'

After several dead-end jobs, including one in which he permanently injured his foot in an industrial accident, in 1929 the Great Depression sent the company he worked for into liquidation. It was then, at the age of just twenty, that Hosking made what at the time seemed a bizarre career move: to try to make a living as a bird photographer. As he explained in his 1970 autobiography, *An Eye for a Bird*:

I was on the dole – during the biggest depression this country had ever known . . . It was the most degrading, depressing period of my life. Yet it also led to the best thing that ever happened to me. I did not know it then, but I was finished with regular employment for ever . . . For me, the depression brought release.

Hosking's opportunity came when an old schoolfriend, by now a sub-editor on a Sunday newspaper, commissioned him to photograph an elephant seal at London Zoo. He took along the four-year-old daughter of a friend, to show the animal's huge size, and was paid two guineas (£2.10, equivalent to about £130 today). From there on, he was a fully-fledged freelance photographer, specialising in birds and wildlife.

Superficially, the title of Eric Hosking's autobiography, *An Eye for a Bird*, refers to the photographer's 'eye': the ability to capture what the great French photographer Henri Cartier-Bresson defined as 'the decisive moment', to create a pleasing – and ideally commercially profitable – image. But the book's title has a much darker double meaning.

On 13 May 1937, Hosking was photographing tawny owls at their nest in rural mid-Wales, using a hide erected on top of a wooden platform. That night, leaving the hide after a frustrating session during which he had not managed to photograph the birds at all, he heard voices nearby. Concerned that his valuable photographic equipment might be vandalised or stolen, he headed back towards the platform. Just as he reached the bottom, out of nowhere he felt a heavy object strike his face, and what he described as 'an agonising stab in my left eye'. He soon realised that one of the nesting owls, regarding him as an unwelcome intruder, had dive-bombed him 'with deadly accuracy, sinking a claw deep into the centre of my eye'.

After being examined by a local doctor, he was advised to travel immediately to Moorfields Eye Hospital, 200 miles away in London. If anyone could save the sight of his eye it was the specialist surgeons there.

The operation itself was a success, but two weeks afterwards, the lead surgeon came to Eric's bedside with very bad news. In these days before antibiotics, an infection had set in which might mean he would lose the sight not only in the injured eye, but possibly in the healthy one as well. He was given twenty-four hours to decide whether to have his left eye removed, in order to prevent the very real chance that he might go completely blind, or to take the risk that he would recover without surgery. As Hosking wrote, more than thirty years later:

> It was an awful decision to make. In my profession sight is everything. Obviously I could not risk going blind, yet what good would a one-eyed naturalist-photographer be? It looked as if the career I loved so much was to end. I was twenty-seven.

As he agonised over the decision, a sliver of hope arrived. Hosking's local church minister visited him in hospital, and told him that Walter Higham, a bird photographer he greatly admired, only had one eye. The very next day, the operation to remove the infected eye went ahead.

Eric Hosking's dramatic decision made the front pages of the national newspapers, prompting an outpouring of concern and affection, with hundreds of cards and letters arriving at the hospital from across the nation. As he later reflected, not only did his misfortune bring him more publicity than he had ever known, before or since the accident, but he also sold a great many more photographs.

When Hosking left Moorfields, you might think that, after this traumatic and life-changing experience, he would travel home to convalesce. Instead, the very next day, he headed straight back to Wales. Now wearing a fencing mask as protection, he climbed up to the hide to see and photograph the owls. But the nest was empty; the chicks had already left. As he explained:

> The gamekeepers wanted to shoot the whole owl family, but I implored them not to. The only shooting I wanted was with a camera, and the following year I *did* shoot them – on film. That, I thought, was just – an eye for a bird.

By the time Eric Hosking died in 1991, aged eighty-one, this quiet, modest and supremely talented man had cemented his place as the godfather of bird photography. His family decided to scatter his ashes at Staverton Park, in Northamptonshire: one of his favourite locations, where he would often photograph barn owls. A decade or so later, they returned to do the same with the ashes of his widow, Dorothy. As they did so, their son David – himself a celebrated wildlife photographer – recalled, a barn owl appeared, flying alongside them before melting away into the trees. 'In a lifetime of bird photography', Eric Hosking once wrote, 'owls have brought me the greatest pleasure.'

With such a large global population, and roughly 50,000 pairs of tawny owls living and breeding in Britain, we might perhaps assume that the species is now safe and secure here. But in 2015 the tawny owl was moved to the Amber List of Birds of Conservation Concern, following what appears to be a steady, long-term, population decline. Paradoxically, for such a common and reasonably widespread species, we know far less about its day-to-day life, and especially the hazards it might face, than we do for many other diurnal birds.

It was not until a fairly recent British Trust for Ornithology (BTO) survey, in 2018–19, in which almost 10,000 volunteers collected data about tawny owls, for example, that it was finally confirmed that a key factor in a potential decline in tawny owl numbers is the amount of light in and around its home territory. With increasing urbanisation, and the greater prevalence of artificial light at night, fewer territories are being occupied. Another unexpected problem comes from the increasing number of deer in our woodlands, as they cause damage to the ground vegetation, which has a knock-on effect on the populations of the small mammals on which the owls feed.

Another intriguing factor has since emerged. Because our British race of the tawny owl – *Strix aluco sylvatica* – is so sedentary, and has been separated from the birds found in mainland Europe for the past 8,000 years or so, by the English Channel and North Sea, might it possibly be evolving into a new and separate species? Although this does seem rather unlikely, scientists point to the recent increase in tawny owls hooting – and some hunting – by day. As Jeff Martin comments, 'reflecting on the interesting daylight behaviour of island Britain's tawny owls, perhaps some or all of them may evolve to become diurnal rather than nocturnal raptors.' It's an intriguing thought.

Whether a unique species or not, whenever we hear 'the clamorous owl, that nightly hoots and wonders', of which Shakespeare writes in *A Midsummer Night's Dream*, we are filled with wonder too.

A. Thorburn

Litho. W. Greve, Berlin.

$\frac{1}{3}$

BARN-OWL.

Strix flammea, *Linn.*

4

BARN OWL

When day declining sheds a milder gleam,
What time the may-fly haunts the pool or stream;
When the still owl skims round the grassy mead,
What time the timorous hare limps forth to feed;
Then be the time to steal adown the vale . . .

Gilbert White, *The Natural History of Selborne* (1789)

In early June, 2015, millions of viewers tuned in to *Springwatch*. As always, they enjoyed intimate live images of Britain's wild creatures going about their day-to-day lives, along with fascinating insights into their behaviour from the presenters, Chris Packham and Michaela Strachan. But while watching footage of a barn owl nest, many had a nasty shock. '*Springwatch* serves up some of TV's most tender moments,' the *Daily Mirror* reported the next day, 'but fans have been left horrified by a scene showing a live baby owl being ripped apart by its mum and fed to its siblings.'

It wasn't the first time *Springwatch* had live-streamed such a thing – indeed, it had happened when I'd been involved with the series, when the oldest chick had been filmed picking up and swallowing the smallest whole, in what Bill Oddie had memorably glossed as 'big brother eats little brother'. But now there was social media, and during and after the programme some viewers complained that the footage was far too gruesome to be broadcast before the watershed, when many children were still watching with their parents. Others even compared the sequence to a horrifically violent scene in the fantasy drama series *Game of Thrones* in which one of the characters burns his own daughter alive at the stake.

To be fair to the programme-makers, Michaela Strachan did give a clear warning before the footage was shown, cautioning that 'things take a disturbing turn at the beginning of this film, so I want to warn you things are a little gruesome.' Later that evening, in the programme's spin-off show *Springwatch Unsprung*, Chris Packham robustly defended showing the sequence. 'We can't put our human values on this. If a spider eats a fly, is it any worse? It's the cycle of life. And we did warn people.'

Chris was, of course, quite correct: the behaviour shown was not some outlying event, but part of the birds' normal life cycle. The reason baby barn owls sometimes eat their smaller siblings is a simple case of survival: when a pair begin breeding, they have no idea whether that season will see a glut of voles, or a shortage. If they laid the same number of eggs each spring, then in years when voles are abundant, they would raise fewer chicks than they could have done if they had laid more. So the female usually produces close to the maximum number of eggs the pair can theoretically raise in a good year: sometimes as many as six or seven, occasionally as many as eleven.

If, however, it is a poor year for voles, with lower numbers than usual, the owls will not be able to raise all their chicks to fledging stage. Rather than let them all starve, it makes perfect sense for the older, larger chicks to eat the smaller, younger ones, which would not be able to survive in any case. This also explains why barn owls – like many other owls and day-flying raptors such as eagles – lay their eggs at one- or two-day intervals, and start to incubate them as soon as the first one is laid, rather than waiting (as songbirds do) until the clutch is complete.

The good news is that, during years when food is abundant, the older chicks are far more kind and caring towards their younger siblings. They will even share food with them, in exchange for preening and grooming, though they usually show a preference for those that call louder than the others.

Certainly viewers' ability to post their opinions in real time on Twitter or Facebook was part of the reason the 2015 footage was picked up in the *Daily Mirror*'s hysterical article. But Chris Packham also wondered if viewers – who had never once complained about blue tits feeding thousands of live moth caterpillars to their hungry chicks – were upset because 'it's a cutesy owl'?

Here we get to the nub. Precisely because we tend to regard owls as 'cute', we recoil at seeing this perfectly natural behaviour. We then react in the way we so often do with wild creatures, by applying human moral standards, and anthropomorphic language, such as describing these acts as 'cannibalism'.

The same year *Springwatch* broadcast that infamous scene, the Urban Birder David Lindo launched a nationwide poll to find Britain's Favourite Bird. The robin won by miles, of course, as everyone expected. But in second place, beating such hot favourites as the blackbird, blue tit, wren, mute swan and kingfisher, was the barn owl.

The barn owl – as its name shows – has lived alongside humans for many thousands of years: at least since nomadic peoples first settled down to farm the land, some 10,000 years ago in the Middle East, and about 5,500 years ago in Britain. The remains of barn owls have been found at various ancient human settlements in Britain, including the Iron Age lake village at Glastonbury, which dates back to the third century BC.

This major switch in human history and behaviour, from hunter-gatherer to settled farmer, was definitely good news for barn owls. It provided them not only with plenty of food, from the various rodents living on farmland and in and around farmyards, but also with a place to roost and breed, in the buildings from which they got their name.

As trees, woods and forests were cut down for fuel and timber, and replaced by more open, farmed country, the barn owl continued to thrive. Eventually it became, for a brief period, Britain's commonest owl, although from the middle of the nineteenth century, the barn owl was overtaken by the tawny, which is now by far our commonest owl species.

According to the ornithological historian Simon Holloway, the barn owl's decline was at least partly due to a change in farming practices, to an increasingly industrialised model, and the agricultural depression at the time, along with a rise in gamekeeping. Because of a reduction in grain harvests, the bird's usefulness as a rodent killer became less crucial; during the same period, gamekeepers took to massacring any predator that threatened their precious birds, using guns and the cruel (and now illegal) pole traps, which resulted in a slow and painful death.

1. *Mochudo* . 2. *y* 3. *Lechuzas* .

This widespread slaughter continued for decades, even though barn owls rarely, if ever, take young pheasants or partridges; as George Orwell pointed out in his 'As I Please' column for the *Tribune* newspaper as long ago as May 1944:

Under the heading 'We Are Destroying Birds that Save Us,' the *News Chronicle* notes that 'beneficial birds suffer from human ignorance. There is senseless persecution of the kestrel and barn owl. No two species of birds do better work for us.' Unfortunately it isn't even from ignorance. Most of the birds of prey are killed off for the sake of that enemy of

England, the pheasant . . . all birds and animals that are suspected of eating its eggs or chicks are systematically wiped out.

Almost eighty years after Orwell wrote those words, little has
changed: gamekeepers at pheasant shoots still routinely – and often
illegally – massacre predators that might threaten their precious birds.

The rise in popularity of taxidermy, and the display of stuffed birds
in drawing rooms and public buildings such as inns, led to a further
massacre of the species, as William Durban and the Revd Murray
Mathew noted scathingly in *The Birds of Devon*, published in 1892: 'In
every little bird-stuffer's shop the Barn Owl may be numbered by the
half-dozen distorted and caricatured.'

Yet despite this longstanding antipathy from some sectors of the
rural population, barn owls have long been part of the day-to-day lives
of country people. 'This elegant bird mostly frequents the habitations
of man,' George Montagu noted approvingly; 'is rarely found in woods,
but resorts chiefly to barns for the sake of mice, for which reason it is a
welcome guest to the farmer.'

The closeness and longevity of this relationship is obvious from the
proliferation of alternative names in English for the species. In his epic
Thesaurus of Bird Names, the etymologist Michel Desfayes collected no
fewer than forty-one. These included widespread and well-known
names such as white owl, ghost owl, church owl, night owl and screech
owl; and more unusual and localised ones, including billy-white (Norfolk), hissing owl (Somerset and Wiltshire), and my favourite,
monkey-owl (Cheshire), from the superficial resemblance of the barn
owl's face to that of a monkey. The species' scientific name, *Tyto alba*,
translates simply as 'white night-owl'.

These folk names mostly derive from the bird's colour (which,
although actually buffish-yellow and cream, often appears white after

dark), its blood-curdling, screeching sound, and its longstanding connection with ghosts. Indeed, Montagu's contemporary Thomas Bewick – who preferred the name 'yellow owl' – conflated the bird's sound with its spookiness: 'It has obtained the name of Screech Owl from its cries, repeated at intervals, and rendered loud and frightful from the stillness of the night.'

Another major figure of Victorian ornithology, William MacGillivray, observed barn owls at Borthwick Castle, 12 miles south-east of Edinburgh. This impressive medieval structure was built for the Scottish peer Sir William Borthwick in 1430. It was also where in 1567 Mary

Queen of Scots stayed while under siege, with her husband James Hepburn, Earl of Bothwell, before eventually making her escape, dressed as a male page. MacGillivray made an explicit connection with this historical event, when, on hearing a calling barn owl, he wrote, 'If the belief of ghosts had not long ago been extinct among the enlightened at least . . . I had taken that shriek for the cry of the beautiful, guilty, and deservedly miserable queen Mary.'

As well as nesting in farm barns, this species regularly breeds in the towers of castles and churches, and hunts around their grounds. It is no stretch of the imagination to suggest that the sound of its screeching, coming from a tower window in the middle of the night, and often followed by the brief appearance of a ghostly, white figure that would float slowly away into the darkness, might have suggested that the building was indeed haunted by ghosts.

Experienced rural naturalists, of course, knew exactly what they were hearing and seeing. 'We have had, ever since I remember, a pair of white owls that constantly breed under the eaves of this church,' wrote Gilbert White of the familiar behaviour of the barn owls which, along with their ancestors, had lived and bred in the parish church at Selborne since well before his lifetime. 'About an hour before sunset . . . they sally forth in quest of prey, and hunt all round the hedges of meadows and small enclosures.'

A meticulous observer, White also gave us a delightful and characteristically precise account of his experience of watching barn owls hunting at dusk:

We can stand on an eminence and see them beat the fields over like a setting-dog, and often drop down in the grass or corn . . . As they take the prey with their claws, so they carry it in their claws to their nest; but, as the feet are necessary [for landing] they perch first on the roof of the chancel, and shift the mouse from their claws to their bill.

Whenever I come across a hunting barn owl, what usually strikes me is the sheer buoyancy and delicacy of its flight. The large, rounded wings, with those dense, soft feathers, mean it is virtually silent; a real asset when trying to locate and kill prey.

Although barn owls mostly hunt either at dawn or dusk, or during the night itself, they regularly do so by day. Usually this is following a period of rainy weather, when flying has been difficult if not impossible. According to the Victorian collector of weather lore, Richard Inwards, the screech of a barn owl was taken by country people to presage a change in the weather, usually a cold spell or a storm. In their 1945 book *Birds of the Night* Eric Hosking and Cyril Newberry advance the same hypothesis. One problem facing a day-hunting barn owl is that it is more likely to attract attention from diurnal predators, or be mobbed by smaller songbirds.

When not hunting, and especially during the daylight hours, barn owls roost mainly in barns, but I did once flush one from a willow tree on a wetland reserve near my home. Because it was a bright, sunny day, and this was the last place I expected to see a barn owl, I initially mistook its paleness and flashes of yellowish-buff for one of the many cattle egrets that have recently colonised the Somerset Levels. Only as it flew slowly away did I realise its true identity.

Of all Britain's seven species of owls, the barn is without doubt the most familiar to country people; indeed, in many ways it is *the* symbol of the farmed countryside. Yet it is not always easy to find. When I moved down from London to Somerset almost two decades ago, I expected to see barn owls far more often than I actually did, at least initially. It was more than a year before I came across my first, as it emerged from a dilapidated reed-cutter's hut at Noah's Lake on the Avalon Marshes, and it took me a full eight years to find one in my parish. I came across this bird during the daytime, one afternoon when I was driving my children back from school: I noticed it dipping low over a hedge, and then being mobbed by two crows, before it finally flew off.

Since then, my barn owl sightings have risen and fallen year by year, presumably connected to cycles in the local vole population, where numbers tend to rise for between two and four years, and then plummet for a year or two. I usually see them either when I'm driving across the damp and open Tadham and Tealham Moors on the nearby Somerset Levels, or when cycling or walking the dog along the lanes behind my home.

Even now, when I have seen so many here over the years, that unmistakable sight of a pale, glowing figure, drifting towards me like a character in a silent movie, always lifts my spirits. Given that my teenage years as a birder, back in the 1970s, coincided with an all-time low in the UK barn owl population, I'm glad that it appears to have made something of a comeback, even though, as we shall see, it still faces major threats.

That floating flight of barn owls – which, perhaps because of their pale coloration, always looks more effortless than other owl species' – is made possible because of their very specific, and in some ways unique, physiology. The barn owl is one of the lightest owls for its size: although only a few centimetres shorter than a tawny (34 cm compared with 38 cm long), it weighs considerably less, tipping the scales at roughly 300 to 360 gm (rather more for females), less than three-quarters the weight of the tawny owl.

Until recently, the barn owl was – along with the peregrine – the most widespread landbird in the world, one of only a handful of species present in six out of seven of the world's continents (excluding Antarctica). As recently as 2010, the definitive account of UK and Irish bird populations, *The Status of Birds in Britain and Ireland*, described the barn owl as being found very widely across Europe, sub-Saharan Africa, Asia, Australia, and in the New World from the Great Lakes to Tierra del Fuego and the Falklands, and even on Hawaii.

In the 1940s, a handful of barn owls began to turn up in New Zealand, even though the 1,500-km crossing of the Tasman Sea from Australia would appear to be out of the question for the species, which like most owls does not usually fly across large expanses of water. Other theories suggested that they might have hitched a ride on boats. But in the early 1980s another explanation came to light: that the birds – several of which were found near Auckland International Airport – had actually hitched a ride inside the wheel housing of a Boeing 747 airliner. One stowaway still had high reserves of fat, so it could not have migrated, and its stomach contained insects found only in Australia, which meant it could not be an escaped bird.

Those early arrivals did not manage to breed in New Zealand, but then in 2008, the first ever barn owl nest was discovered there. Over the next decade or so, the species managed to colonise North Island, and the population is now estimated to be in the hundreds of pairs. Fortunately, barn owls do not appear to compete for food or nesting sites with the country's only native species of owl, the morepork, and because they appear to have arrived naturally (albeit with some inadvertent human assistance), they are now considered an official native species rather than an invasive pest. They have the added benefit of killing non-native rodents such as rats and mice.

Over the years, I have seen barn owls at many far-flung points on the globe. I remember leaving a pizza restaurant by the beach in Israel's Red Sea resort of Eilat, when one unexpectedly materialised out of the darkness. Another time, while I was birding in a remote part of eastern Trinidad, a very dark-breasted bird emerged into bright daylight from a ruined building. And on a night-time walk in tropical north

Queensland, in search of nocturnal possums and bandicoots, I saw one appear briefly alongside the forest edge.

But a couple of years ago I discovered, to my surprise, that the 'barn owl' had been split into three separate species: the western barn owl *Tyto alba* (in Europe and Africa), the American barn owl *Tyto furcata* (throughout the Americas), and the eastern barn owl *Tyto javanica* (across Asia and Australasia). I didn't know whether to be pleased that I added two new species to my 'world list' – the birds I saw in Trinidad and Queensland – or sad that the barn owl has lost its status as the world's most widespread and cosmopolitan owl (now replaced by the short-eared – see Chapter 6). To be honest, as with so many of these recent 'splits', based on differences in DNA between different populations, I'm inclined to point out that barn owls are always unmistakably barn owls, whatever the scientists might say.

Whether one, two or three species, barn owls are one of the world's most successful members of their tribe, for a number of reasons. First, their long history alongside human beings means they can swiftly adapt to rapid changes in their environment, and take advantage of the plentiful food on farmland (as long as they avoid being killed by rodenticides and other poisons). They also feed on a large variety of often-abundant prey, including small birds, bats and frogs as well as small mammals, and have the ability to nest in a wide range of different sites, especially man-made ones (though they would originally, of course, have nested in rocks and crevices). As Robert Mudie so eloquently observed in the early nineteenth century, 'Instead of spurning the society of man, it courts the neighbourhood of his dwelling.'

One of the most obvious differences between the 'true' or 'typical' owls from the family Strigidae, and barn owls from Tytonidae, is the characteristically dark, heart-shaped disk that surrounds and frames the pale face of the latter. This is especially obvious when a perched bird looks right back at you, as it will often do, before taking flight on those ultra-quiet wings.

Barn owls are also a different colour and pattern to our other owls: not just paler, but less streaky and mottled, and so plainer, than the rest. The BTO's Mike Toms, in the Collins New Naturalist *Owls*, describes them as being 'white underneath and washed with golden buff above ... [with] an intricate overlay of silver-grey markings', which are usually only visible when you get very close. Males are generally white below, while females have heavier and darker speckling, sometimes buff in colour, across their underparts.

Studies by scientists in the Department of Ecology and Evolution at the University of Lausanne, Switzerland, led by Professor Alexandre Roulin, suggest that barn owls might become more successful hunters during clear nights with a full moon, especially if they are birds with whiter underparts. Whereas you might assume that birds of prey would benefit from a camouflaged plumage when pursuing their intended victim, it appears that barn owls actually want to be seen.

The researchers discovered this by looking at historical data on the owls' hunting success, which showed that during a full moon the whiter individuals brought more food back to their nest. They then confirmed their hypothesis by simulating attacks on voles using stuffed owls, some with dark underparts, others pale. To their surprise, the voles 'froze' – stopped moving to try to hide from the predator – for five seconds longer when a white owl flew overhead, suggesting that they were being dazzled by the paler bird. Indeed, the researchers went one step further, describing the voles as 'terrified' by these 'ghosts'. Perhaps the same applies to human observers who, on seeing a pale owl emerge from the darkness, are mesmerised into believing it is not a bird, but a ghostly apparition.

RP-P-BJ- 1419

A further reason for barn owls' almost supernatural aura is their singular sound. They may not be quite as vocal as tawny or little owls, but they make up for it with their wide range of calls, generally uttered during the breeding season. When you first hear a barn owl call, you can be forgiven for assuming you are listening not to a bird, but some kind of scary spectre.

Their varied repertoire, made by both males and females, includes a tuneless screeching, rather like fingernails being scraped across a blackboard, and described by the Welsh poet R. S. Thomas as its 'night-strangled cry'. There is also a warning scream, used to sound alarm; anxiety and distress calls; a loud hiss – used in defence against a predator or intruder close to the nest or chicks; a snore, a series of tweets and twitters, and a gentler, purring sound, used to communicate with their mate. In Reginald Bosworth Smith's succinct summation, 'The white owl screeches, snaps, snorts, snores, squawks, hisses; but it is now, I think, established that he never hoots.'

Shakespeare's several mentions of the screeching of the barn owl always signify something sinister. In *Macbeth*, 'it was the owl that shrieked, the fatal bellman,' preceding the murder of Duncan, following which Lady Macbeth hears the owl scream again at the moment of his death. Another owl is said to have shrieked at the birth of one of the characters in *Henry VI Part 3*, while barn owls shriek at key moments in *A Midsummer Night's Dream* and *Richard III*. In 'The Grave', published in 1743, a lesser-known poet, the Scot Robert Blair, also associated the call of the barn owl with impending doom:

> Again! The screech-owl shrieks, ungracious sound!
> I'll hear no more, it makes one's blood run chill.

The one time when barn owls make no sound at all is when they are hunting their rodent prey. Even when you stand very close to a wild or captive bird in flight, you can hear absolutely nothing. The comb-like serrations along the front edge of its wings, and the soft fringe on the back edge, that characterise owls which hunt low over the ground, allow the barn owl to float silently over long grass and greatly reduce the chance of disturbing its prey (small mammals such as mice and voles have excellent hearing), and also enable it to hear any movements of its hidden victim. The lower wing loading that comes with the barn owls' long, broad wings, compared with other species of a similar size like crows, doves or pigeons – the added buoyancy created by spreading their weight across a wider area – means they fly not only silently, but also very slowly; again, increasing their chances of detecting hidden prey.

As well as hunting and feeding across farmland, barn owls often make their nest in barns and other farm buildings. Some pairs roost together throughout the autumn and winter, frequently calling to one another, and even occasionally mutually preening. They are very faithful to one another and to the place where they nest: even passing on their territory down the family line. They and their descendants may use the same nest for at least twenty or thirty years, and perhaps as long as seventy years or more, as Gilbert White reported from the church at Selborne. And most stay on or around their breeding territory all year round.

In his short poem 'Evening', White's successor John Clare paints a graphic portrait of a barn owl emerging from its farmyard refuge at sunset, as dusk falls over the Northamptonshire countryside:

> Barn door fowls have gone to bed
> Though the sun is two yards high
> Ere it reach the top lands head
> That takes days lamp from out the sky . . .
>
> Now the owl on wheaten wing
> And white hood scowling o'er his eyes
> Jerking with a sudden spring
> Through three-cornered barn hole flies.

Although barn owls do indeed often nest in barns, they also favour a range of other nest sites, including other (often disused or ruined) farm buildings, holes in trees, cliffs, mines and quarries. They will often prefer artificial nest boxes over natural sites.

Like other birds, they will sometimes choose very strange places to make their nest. Gilbert White recalled a local dovecote being 'infested by a pair of white owls, which made great havoc among the young pigeons'. The owner of the dovecote, he went on to reveal, shot one of the owls, whereupon the other found a new mate, so then he killed both the new pair, following which 'the annoyance ceased'. White also wrote of a very peculiar case of a swallow building its own nest 'on the wings and body of an owl that happened by accident to hang dead and dry from the rafter of a barn'.

The average date for the female laying her first egg – and thus beginning the incubation cycle – used to be 9 May; this has now shifted forward by more than three weeks, to 17 April, owing to rising temperatures caused by the climate crisis. A typical finished clutch contains between four and six eggs – almost round, and of a dirty-white colour, speckled lightly with reddish-brown – but up to eleven have been recorded in a single nest.

The incubation period – carried out entirely by the female, who is fed by the male throughout – lasts for thirty-two days. After the chicks have hatched (asynchronously, because of the delay in starting to incubate the later eggs), they do not fledge until between seven-and-a-half and nine weeks afterwards. Soon after birth, before they are covered in pale, fluffy down, they look rather scrawny, leading Mike Toms to describe them as 'particularly unattractive during their first few days of life'.

Once they are fully fledged, in the UK at least, young barn owls tend to stay fairly close to where they were born; elsewhere, they often move considerable distances: between 50 and 100 km in continental Europe, and as far as 320 km in North America, where one travelled an incredible 1,760 km from its birthplace. Like most birds, young barn owls have a far lower than even chance of surviving their first year: only just over one in three manage to reach that milestone. If they do, adults will typically live for four years, although one ringed bird, recovered in 2016, reached the age of nearly fifteen years and four months.

Death may occur during long periods of wet or very cold, snowy weather, when the birds struggle to find food, because their soft feathers soon get waterlogged if they fly in the rain, and snow on the ground can prevent them from finding food. They may also fall victim to a predator such as a peregrine, buzzard or even a tawny owl.

In their authoritative 1982 monograph *The Barn Owl*, D. S. Bunn, A. B. Warburton and R. D. S. Wilson list a number of other causes of death, including collisions with road vehicles, overhead wires and power cables; a litany of parasites; and, perhaps most surprisingly, drowning. It seems that barn owls can come to grief either when losing their balance and tipping forward while drinking from a source of water, or possibly by becoming confused by seeing their own reflection in the water, following which they attempt to attack it, become water-logged and sink rapidly to their death.

The status of the barn owl in Britain is surprisingly hard to fathom, partly because, as with all owls, its nocturnal habits mean it can easily be missed during surveys, and partly because the population naturally waxes and wanes with the regular cycle of vole numbers.

Barn owls breed across much of our lowland countryside, with their main strongholds in East Anglia, Lincolnshire and the Scottish Borders, but are absent from the upland areas of England, Scotland and Wales, the offshore islands of Scotland, and most of Northern Ireland. The current best estimates of the UK population are between 10,000 and 12,000 breeding pairs; considerably higher than the late 1980s, when there were just 4,500 pairs, numbers having fallen dramatically after the Second World War.

The reasons for the barn owl's post-war decline are sadly familiar and predictable: a loss of grassland habitat; the impact of agricultural chemicals, especially rodenticides which reduced the abundance of their prey; the rise in road traffic, resulting in an increase in collisions between vehicles and these low-flying birds; and the disappearance of nesting sites as barns were converted into homes. Ironically, one holiday home in rural Cheshire lists barn owls as among its visitor attractions – 'In the evening . . . keep an eye out for the barn owls as there are several mating pairs in the area' – even though the property appears to be a converted farm building, no longer available as a home for owls.

Fortunately, a number of initiatives to reverse the long-term decline of barn owls appear to be working very well. Releasing birds bred in captivity, and providing field margins with longer grass on many farms, have helped increase numbers, while a run of mild winters, with little or no snow across much of southern Britain since the winters of 2010–11 and 2011–12, has also helped.

There are also some really imaginative and effective local schemes. A few years ago, Chris Sperring, who was deservedly awarded an MBE for his efforts to promote the conservation of owls, launched a project to put up a barn owl nest box in every single parish of my home county of Somerset. By the end of 2014, with support from the Hawk and Owl

Trust and the Somerset Wildlife Trust, he had succeeded, with a total of 334 boxes installed. In neighbouring Dorset, a similar scheme run by the county council has also led to a rise in barn owl numbers. Despite these efforts, however, barn owls are still not as common a sight in Somerset as they should be.

The last word about barn owls should go to the authors of what, despite being over forty years old, remains the most detailed book-length monograph on the species, *The Barn Owl*. 'Over the years', they note in the preface, 'it has become obvious to us that most of our relatives, friends and casual acquaintances have come to regard us as mentally deranged as a result of our long study of the Barn Owl: we are forever being asked why we do it.'

They go on to list the downsides of studying this elusive and mostly nocturnal bird: 'We do lose inordinate amounts of sleep, we do get eaten alive by a varied assortment of biting flies, gnats, mosquitoes and midges, we are frequently exposed to the vagaries of the British climate . . . [and] we do spend long hours when absolutely nothing happens.' But they continue to do so for the same reason their American predecessors Julian K. Porter and John A. Gillespie did back in 1925: 'The study of the barn owl is certain to furnish countless thrills, many a quickening of the pulse, and a greater appreciation of this . . . benefactor of mankind.' No one who has ever watched a barn owl hunting – if only for a few moments – will disagree.

5

LITTLE OWL

The owl of Minerva [the Little Owl] spreads its wings
only with the coming of the dusk.

Georg Wilhelm Friedrich Hegel,
The Philosophy of Right (1820)

Charles Waterton (1782–1865) was a Victorian explorer, a noted eccentric and, most importantly of all, one of the world's first environmentalists.

As an explorer, he wrote about his pioneering travels in the New World in his celebrated 1825 book *Wanderings in South America*. His eccentricity was the stuff of legend: to confuse his guests he would dress as a scarecrow and sit in trees, or pretend to be his own butler. But it is his pioneering role as an environmentalist that really deserves praise. In the 1820s, he turned his estate into the world's earliest known nature reserve, and invented the first nest box for birds. Waterton also played a small but significant part in the arrival of the smallest British member of the owl family to our shores. Following a visit to Rome in 1842, he brought back an unusual cargo – five little owls – and released the birds into the grounds of his country estate, Walton Hall in West Yorkshire, hoping they would feed on garden pests.

Before this date, the species was not generally found in Britain, though in *The Feathered Tribes of the British Isles*, published almost a decade earlier in 1834, Robert Mudie wrote that

It is rarely seen in England, and if it breeds in the country its nest has not hitherto been met with. When seen, it is generally in the autumn, so that it may be blown across [the English Channel] in the course of its autumnal migration.

The Handbook of British Birds (1938–41) suggests that perhaps twenty records which predate Waterton's releases were genuine vagrants from continental Europe. The early-nineteenth-century ornithologist Thomas Bewick mentioned several vagrant little owls shot around parts of England, while his contemporary George Montagu described it as 'a very rare species in England', adding, 'It is said to fly by day, and to give chace [sic] to small birds; but its principal food is mice.' Mudie also notes that the species lives in 'the vicinity of human dwellings [and is] an industrious and successful mouser'.

Despite Charles Waterton's best efforts, his quintet of little owls did not survive for long, although one is said to have travelled as far as Derby, some 50 miles away. About the same time, another was shot in West Sussex, which is more likely to have been a genuine migrant from across the Channel.

More than three decades later, from the mid-1870s onwards, the full-scale introductions of little owls to Britain finally began. The first such attempt, by another landowner and ornithologist, Edmund Meade-Waldo, took place on his country estate of Stonewall Park, near Edenbridge in Kent. Perhaps inspired by Waterton's earlier efforts, between 1874 and 1900 Meade-Waldo released about ninety birds here.

Soon afterwards, at his country estate in Oundle, Northamptonshire, the aristocrat Lord Lilford also released a number of little owls, which he had imported from the Netherlands via the London bird markets. The first successful nest with chicks was recorded there in April 1889. Over the next two decades, little owls were introduced to a number of locations across England, from Sussex, Essex and Hampshire in the south, to Yorkshire in the north.

Most commentators now believe that the birds released by Meade-Waldo and Lord Lilford kick-started the successful establishment of little owls in Britain. This happened surprisingly rapidly, helped by the fact that this species occupies a very specific ecological niche and so does not compete with any of our native raptors. As the ornithologist Richard Fitter put it in his 1959 book *The Ark in our Midst*, little owls did so well in Britain because there was 'a vacancy for a small, diurnal, mainly insect-eating bird of prey'.

By the start of the twentieth century, wandering little owls were being recorded as far afield as Somerset, while during the 1910s and 1920s they began to breed across most of southern England, East Anglia, Wales, the Midlands and parts of northern England. By the time *The Handbook* was published, at the start of the Second World War, they were regularly seen as far north as Durham and Northumberland, even with a few records from Scotland.

Today, according to the BTO, the estimated UK breeding population of little owls is between 2,350 and 4,900 (mean figure 3,600) pairs. They are mostly found across lowland rural England, with a few breeding in west and north Wales and the Scottish borders, although, like tawny owls, they are entirely absent as breeding birds from Ireland, where there has only been a handful of records.

The little owl's main stronghold is the arable farmland of East Anglia and south-east England, where they are a regular sight as they perch on fence posts, barn roofs and on the branches of oak trees. Where I live in Somerset, and indeed in the West Country in general, little owls are fairly thin on the ground. Fortunately, however, I regularly hear – and sometimes see – them, in and around my long, wooded garden on the edge of the Somerset Levels.

My very first sighting here was in the summer of 2007, a year after we moved down from London, in the allotment across the road. This was thanks to the kindness of my neighbour Mick, who noticed one perched in a hedge one hot August afternoon, and called me over. Only when he pointed it out did I notice this small, plump bird, with its bright custard-yellow eyes, looking back at me.

Globally, the little owl is a very common and widespread bird

throughout the warm and temperate regions of Europe, North Africa and Asia. Its range extends from the Iberian Peninsula and Morocco in the west, to China and Korea in the east, north to Britain and Denmark, and south as far as the Arabian Peninsula and Horn of Africa. The global population, which comprises thirteen recognised subspecies, is estimated at between five and fifteen *million* birds, meaning that the conservation organisation BirdLife International classifies the species as being of 'Least Concern'.

Little owls were also introduced to South Island, New Zealand, back in the early twentieth century, when over 200 birds were shipped over from Germany (hence an alternative name for the species there, 'German owl'). According to Christopher Lever's *Naturalised Birds of the World*, this was supposedly in order to control house sparrows and other introduced species, which were rapidly becoming pests on farm crops. It remains the only raptor species ever introduced to New Zealand. Lever notes that the little owl continues to thrive there, to the detriment of several native species of songbird, and also, through competition for food (and unlike the barn owl), threatening the country's only surviving native owl, the slightly larger, and darker brown, morepork.

Back home, a century or more after they were first released here, most people now consider little owls to be a genuinely native British bird. This is in stark contrast to other so-called 'alien' species, such as the Canada goose and rose-ringed parakeet, which usually provoke more antagonistic views. In the case of the goose and parakeet, this may be down to their brash behaviour, but it is also surely due to their distant origins in North America and Asia, leading us to regard them as somehow more foreign than the 'European' little owl.

That the little owl originates so close to our shores – and arguably would have been here anyway without the relatively recent existence of a marine barrier between Britain and continental Europe – possibly makes us more inclined to accept it as a true Brit. And perhaps they were indeed once living here, sometime in the distant past, only to disappear later on. The ornithologist and broadcaster James Fisher suggested that bones of this species were found in Late Ice Age deposits – between 100,000 and 25,000 years ago. The latest archaeological studies prove that the little owl was definitely present in the ancient fossil record, dating back one-and-a-half to two-and-a-half million years; in which case we might perhaps argue that the little owls released by those Victorian ornithologists were not so much introductions, but very delayed *reintroductions*!

The traditional association of owls with wisdom is, for the little owl, confirmed in its scientific name: *Athene noctua*. This is derived from the Greek goddess (and daughter of Zeus) Athene – also known as Athena – the goddess of wisdom and military victory. Athene is the Greek equivalent of Minerva, the Roman goddess of handicrafts, the professions, the arts, and war.

As with so many ancient myths, the origins of the connection between this small owl and the goddess, who gave her name to the city of Athens, are somewhat vague. Some suggest that owls' ability to see – especially in the dark – gave them the reputation for wisdom; Athene, meanwhile had the gift of seeing into the future. But the simple fact that little owls are a very common bird around Athens – and, often being diurnal in their habits, are more visible than other owls – may also have been a contributory factor.

Whatever the reason, little owls (and other owl species) frequently feature on Ancient Greek vases, coins and other relics. At the naval battle of Salamis, in 480 BC, the sudden appearance of owls was taken, not as the usual portent of doom, but as Athena's blessing on the troops, as was also the case in a later victory over Carthage, by Syracuse, in 310 BC.

According to the historian Diodorus of Sicily, the owls were released deliberately to boost morale. Most famously, a terracotta vase on display in New York's Metropolitan Museum of Art, which has been dated to between 490 and 480 BC, and attributed to the craftsman the 'Brygos Painter', shows Athena holding a helmet and looking directly towards a hovering little owl.

The Greek philosopher and prototype naturalist Aristotle, writing in the fourth century BC, was the first person to create a metaphor of the 'night owl' as an analogy with the human mind. More than two millennia later, the German philosopher Hegel contrasted, in the epigraph to this chapter, the little owl's wisdom with the inability of human beings to interpret the world: 'The owl of Minerva spreads its wings only with the coming of the dusk.' Hegel means that we are only able to understand a historical event with hindsight, by which time, of course, it is too late. It would be churlish, perhaps, to point out that although little owls are mainly nocturnal, they also fly frequently during daylight hours, so his argument is based on a rather dubious understanding of the species and its behaviour.

As its name suggests, the little owl is by far the smallest member of its family in Britain. At around 21–23 cm long, and with a 54–58 cm wingspan, it is roughly the same length as a starling or song thrush, although at between 140 and 220 gm it is about twice the weight of those slimmer, lighter songbirds.

In Europe, however, there are a number of even smaller members of the family, including three species of scops owls, Tengmalm's owl, and by far the smallest, the pygmy owl, which at 15–19 cm long, and weighing just 50–77 gm, is barely bigger than a house sparrow (hence its Swedish name *sparfuggla*, meaning 'sparrow owl').

Because of their small size, and rather plump and dumpy appearance, little owls are not usually confused with any of our native owls, or indeed with any other common British bird. They have a distinctive grey-brown plumage, speckled with white spots on their crown, back and wings, brown streaks down their breast, and a pale cream belly. The bill is grey and curved, and their feet are strong and powerful, with thick feathering around the legs. With their distinctive, bounding flight they look like a plump, round-winged woodpecker.

The little owl's head is broad and flat, with white eyebrows and a white collar surrounding a pair of dark black eyes with yellow irises, giving them a rather stern, even fierce, expression as they look back at you. But be alert: the little owl has a very similar coloration and pattern on the back of its head, so that, when seen from behind, it looks as if it is facing you. This is a clever evolutionary strategy, to fool predators into thinking the owl is staring straight back at them, when it is actually looking in the opposite direction.

Little owls are one of the classic birds of our lowland, farmed countryside. Each pair holds a territory – the male usually for the whole of his life. This is made up of a patchwork of varied habitats, including hedgerows, fields, farmyards, grassland and woodland, with some also straying into urban or suburban areas, including larger gardens.

The actual size of the little owl's home range – where it seeks its food – can vary considerably: from less than 2 hectares, when there is a diversity of different habitats, to more than 12 hectares on less varied farmland. The more diverse the territory, the more food is available, so the higher the chance of successful breeding. The larger the territory, the greater the chances of an encounter with another male, often resulting in a struggle as the resident bird tries to eject the unwelcome intruder.

Little owls hunt a wide range of prey items, including small mammals such as mice, rats, shrews, voles, moles, and even baby rabbits.

They frequently catch songbirds: the nineteenth-century nature writer Robert Mudie reported seeing one using a specific technique to hunt swallows, 'opposing a direct flight to their wheeling one, and endeavouring to meet them as they come round'. However, their small size means they can also thrive on smaller prey, especially large insects and other invertebrates – for example, worms, crickets, grasshoppers and beetles. Analysis of their pellets has revealed that mammals make up between one-quarter and one-half of their diet; about the same ratio as insects and other invertebrates.

I have sometimes come across a little owl perching on the lower branches of an oak tree, or on a fence post or gate, its eyes glowing in the sunshine. It isn't sunbathing, but on the lookout for any sign of movement on the ground below: the scurrying of a vole in the grass, perhaps, or the sudden appearance of a beetle or worm. As soon as it spots a potential victim, it drops down onto the ground and, with a swift movement of the head, grabs it with its beak, before flying back to the perch to consume the unfortunate creature. If little owls have already fed, they may hide (or 'cache') any surplus prey in a convenient hiding place, to eat at their leisure. As Robert Mudie also noted, 'It is an industrious and successful mouser, and though its wings are not very long, it is more quick in the use of them than some of the larger species.'

As opportunistic feeders, little owls will alter their hunting strategy depending on the season and weather, and cache food when it is plentiful. In summer, they may take large beetles such as maybugs, while at any time of year, if it rains, they focus on earthworms as these emerge onto the surface of the soil. According to the BTO, when feeding on worms, 'this diminutive owl . . . is occasionally observed to fall over backwards when unexpectedly successful in trying to extract large individuals from the ground'. That would be worth seeing!

Little owls do occasionally take advantage of an abundant but unlikely food source, as on the islands of Skomer and Skokholm, off the Pembrokeshire coast in West Wales. Both are well known for migrating songbirds in spring and autumn (Skokholm was the site of Britain's first ever bird observatory, founded in 1933), and especially their globally important populations of seabirds, including storm petrels and Manx shearwaters. During the summer months, when they breed, these small and vulnerable birds usually return to the islands under cover of darkness, to avoid being picked off by the fearsome and predatory herring and great black-backed gulls which hang around the shearwaters' and petrels' nesting burrows, and try to snatch and kill the adults as they return with food for their hungry chicks.

In July 1936, soon after the bird observatory on Skokholm was set up, its founder Ronald Lockley discovered that a smaller and far more unexpected predator was also wreaking havoc on the island's population of European storm petrels. 'We found a [little owl] nest . . . in a rabbit burrow, with two tiny owl chicks and a larder of nearly 200 corpses of storm petrels, the majority with only the head removed!'

As Lockley described in his 1983 book *Flight of the Storm Petrel*, he and his colleagues made the tricky decision to shoot the pair of little owls, which had only colonised the island a decade or so earlier. From then onwards, they began a policy of 'shooting or banishing' any owls they came across, 'preferring to protect our petrels rather than encourage this acclimatised importation from Europe', as he described them. In recent years, little owls have occasionally bred on Bardsey Island, further north along the Welsh coast, where a pair was found preying on Manx shearwaters.

During the 1930s, a few decades after the species was first introduced to Britain, a group of eminent scientists suggested that little owls – then derogatorily dubbed 'Frenchies' because of their continental origin – might be having a detrimental effect on the chicks of domestic poultry and gamebirds. After a thorough inquiry, however, this accusation was proved groundless. Indeed, as key predators of potentially harmful invertebrates and introduced species of rodents on farmland, little owls are generally considered a valued addition to our avifauna. As Christopher Lever points out, 'of all the sixty or so alien vertebrates [mostly birds and mammals] naturalised in Britain, the little owl is the only one that is actually beneficial to man.'

Like most owls, when it comes to breeding, this species is monogamous, with the male and female remaining faithful to one another for the whole of their reproductive life (usually from the age of one year to about three years old), unless of course one of them dies prematurely. For first-time breeders, pair-bonding usually begins as early as February, when they start to call frequently to one another.

I usually hear their distinctive call in my garden from this time of year onwards. The sound is superficially similar to the *kee-wick* or *tu-whit* of a female tawny owl, but more monosyllabic, less tuneful and, to my ears, more petulant in tone. When little owls breed, as they often do, in the orchard next door, they will continue to utter this strident call during the evening and night, throughout the rest of the breeding season.

Like many other owls and birds of prey, when courting, the male little owl will bring gifts of food to his mate, helping to keep her healthy and consolidate the bond between them. For the next two months or so, the pair will spend more and more time together, investigating potential nesting sites, which are generally in a cavity of a tree, wall, building, haystack, cliff or quarry. Like the burrowing owl of the Americas (see Chapter 9), some even nest in old rabbit burrows.

Once they have chosen the nest site, the female will immediately begin laying her clutch, usually of three or four – but sometimes two, or as many as five or more – almost round, matt white eggs, generally on alternate days. Like barn owls, she will start to incubate her eggs long before the clutch is complete (usually after the second egg has been laid), so that the chicks hatch a few days apart from one another, from roughly four weeks later. As with the barn owl, this is a sensible evolutionary tactic, to make sure that if food is scarce, the oldest and strongest chicks will survive; if there is a glut of prey, probably all will. In some years, when food is especially abundant, little owls might even raise two broods of young.

The female does all the incubation duties, although the male is busy finding food for her and, once the chicks hatch, the whole family. Later, as the chicks grow larger and stronger, both parents will hunt and bring back food for them. The youngsters stay in the nest for about seven weeks, even though at this stage they are still unable to fly. After they leave the nest, they hang around the area for some time, at least until they can fly properly, before eventually dispersing during the autumn to between 10 and 20 kilometres away.

One especially hot summer a few years ago, a newly-fledged brood of four baby little owls regularly perched on the roof of the converted barn just west of our home, where each evening they were momentarily silhouetted against the setting sun. As dusk fell, they would begin that incessant call, sounding rather like a lapwing crossed with a small and yappy dog. For the rest of the night, when not away hunting, they would move around between the top of the barn and our own roof, calling constantly.

I was of course delighted they had chosen to perch so close to our bedroom. One member of my family, however, took a very different view. My son Charlie, who in summer always sleeps with his bedroom window wide open, was disturbed by the commotion to the point of suggesting – in jest – that he would shoot the birds with an air rifle.

Fortunately, for both him and the owls, he eventually got used to the nightly chorus and managed to get some sleep.

He is not the only person to have been disturbed by the little owl's call. 'When settled it emits a louder and sharper cry,' reported William MacGillivray, 'so distinct that one might take it for a person calling out . . . [Comte] Buffon says that one of his people was so deceived by the cry of one at night, that he went to the window, and called out, "Who is down there?"'

Young little owls face an uphill struggle to survive, with fewer than one in three managing to reach their first birthday. Once they gain independence from their parents, they are at high risk of starvation, especially during hard winters, when ice or snow make it difficult to hunt for food. They are also in danger of being predated, by everything from stoats and weasels to foxes, squirrels, buzzards, sparrowhawks and peregrines, and even other species of owls. And, as David Ballance notes in *A History of the Birds of Somerset*, little owls are probably killed by collisions with motor vehicles at least as often as barn owls, but because of their small size this is rarely recorded. If they do survive to breed, they are likely to live for a total of three years or so; one ringed bird, re-trapped in 2016, had managed to survive in the wild for nearly fourteen years.

According to the UK Little Owl Project and the BTO, however, the UK's population is in freefall, having dropped by almost two-thirds over a twenty-five-year period, with the decline accelerating since the turn of the millennium. Its range has also contracted, especially in south-west England and Wales – my fellow birder Kevin Cox tells me that there are now only fifty breeding pairs in Devon, and none at all in Cornwall.

Along with other British owls – and indeed so many familiar birds of our countryside – it depends for long-term success on the way we manage the farmed countryside, which in recent decades has not been looked after very well at all. Intensive farming reduces their breeding habitats – by the loss of farmland trees and hedgerows – and their prey, because of the over-use of chemical pesticides, especially insecticides and rodenticides. The current climate crisis, and especially the unpredictable (and more frequent) spells of very hot and dry, (or conversely damp and wet) weather, are also affecting little owl survival rates.

As with all farmland birds, including the barn owl, the best way to reverse the decline in little owl numbers would be to create less intensive, more prey-rich habitat, especially rough grassland; include seed mixes to encourage small birds and mammals to feed on arable crops; and retain mature trees with natural cavities where the birds can nest. Alongside that, we can give the birds a helping hand by putting up nest boxes. If the current obsession with high-yield, high-intensity agriculture can be reversed, little owl numbers will bounce back fairly rapidly. If not, they will undoubtedly continue to decline.

6

LONG-EARED AND SHORT-EARED OWLS

This one is more loquacious on the hillside
at night than the nightingale from the slope.
During the day it doesn't shift its head
from a big hollow tree, wise behaviour.

Dafydd ap Gwilym, 'The Owl' (*c.* 1350)

It was a warm, sunny August afternoon; too warm for most birds, although a handful of swallows were hawking for insects in the deep blue sky, above the River Huntspill on the Somerset coast. I wasn't even here to look for birds; at least, not primarily. Instead, I had my eyes down, searching carefully through the long, dry grass for late summer butterflies: skippers, coppers, blues and browns. And then, without warning, a bird appeared out of the hawthorn hedge nearby. It was clearly an owl, but which one? It was obviously too dark for a barn owl, so my first thought was a tawny. And, on a quick view, the bird's rounded wings and richly mottled, dark chestnut-brown plumage suggested that.

But as I watched it fly away, something did not feel quite right. For a start, the bird looked far too small and compact. On the very few occasions I have seen a tawny owl flying during the daytime, it has appeared huge, with a characteristically floppy flight. This bird, by contrast, looked much smaller and slimmer. Then I noticed rusty-orange spots on the upperwings.

As the seconds ticked past, as if in slow motion, my brain began to click into action. Meanwhile, the swallows, which before the owl appeared had been twittering softly to one another, went berserk, increasing the volume and intensity of their alarm calls, while flying as close as they dared to the invader in their midst. As the harassed bird fled across the river and plunged into the willows on the other side, never to be seen again, I finally worked out its identity. It was, of course, a long-eared owl – the first I had ever seen in Somerset.

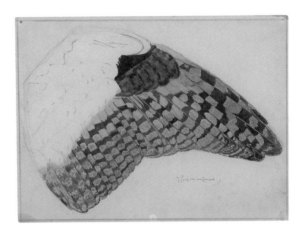

It was also the first long-eared owl I had ever seen in flight, which partly explained why I had struggled to identify it. What I had forgotten was that, when long-eared owls take to the wing, they lower their prominent ear tufts (not actually ears, but feathers); hence this bird's uncharacteristically round-headed appearance.

I had seen long-eared owls a few times, in Britain and abroad, but always at their daytime roost, where the birds sit quietly and unobtrusively in trees, as if taking part in a collective meditation session. They are hoping to avoid any attention until night falls, when they can resume their nocturnal life cycle once again.

Superficially the long-eared owl, and its larger, bulkier cousin the short-eared owl – which I have treated together here, to point out their similarities and contrasts – are fairly alike. Looking at their pictures in

SHORT-EARED OWL.
Asio brachyotus (Forster).

a field guide you might initially struggle to tell the two species apart, were it not for the former bird's longer ear tufts, and deep orange, rather than yellow, irises – and its distinctive plumage, beautifully described by the naturalist Brett Westwood as being 'as richly patterned as a Persian carpet'.

But although the two species are closely related, being two of the eight or nine species of owl in the genus *Asio* (from a Latin word meaning 'eared', coined by the Roman writer and early naturalist Pliny the Younger), their habits, behaviour and lifestyle could hardly be more different.

Whereas the long-eared is, along with the much commoner tawny owl, the most nocturnal member of its family, rarely emerging during daylight hours, the short-eared is one of our most diurnal owls, often hunting during the middle of the day. Whereas the long-eared owl lives, breeds and hunts in dense forests and plantations, and on nearby heaths, the short-eared prefers open moorland during the breeding season, and coastal marshes or rough grasslands during the autumn and winter.

And whereas the long-eared owl is a prime candidate for being the most elusive of all British breeding birds, the short-eared is – if not exactly easy to see, especially following a steady decline in recent years – a bird you are likely to be able to find if you make the effort. That's especially if you live in or travel to northern England or Scotland during the spring and summer, or visit its windswept coastal haunts in autumn and winter.

Portions of outer webs of 1st primaries of : 3, Short-eared Owl, 4, Long-eared Owl.
5, Nestling in down, 6, Juvenile, of Long-eared Owl.
[*Face p.* 92.]

The short-eared owl is slightly larger, heavier and bulkier than the long-eared: a couple of centimetres longer, at 37–39 cm (compared with the long-eared at 35–37 cm), and weighing an average of 330 gm compared with 290 gm. When perched, the short-eared looks plumper and broader in body, whereas the long-eared appears long and thin, this appearance accentuated by those prominent ear tufts, and what has been described as a 'teddy-bear face', as opposed to the short-eared's 'cat face'. The short-eared owl also has ear tufts on the top of its rounded head, but they are so small as to be hard to see unless you get a very close look at a perched bird.

Like many species of owl, both sport a mottled brown and buff plumage, the short-eared usually appearing paler (especially in flight), with mid-brown shading to the wings, and dark brown (almost black) wingtips. When in flight, both tend to hold their long, narrow wings in a shallow V-shape, beating them up and down in a characteristically jerky, almost bat-like flight action. Thus, although at first sight it is possible to mistake them for a harrier or other bird of prey, their identity as owls is usually fairly easy to work out.

Neither species is prominent in folklore, probably because they do not live so closely alongside human beings as barn and tawny owls. Nevertheless, according to Lewis Loyd's miscellany of folklore *Bird Facts and Fallacies*, published in the 1920s, in Belgium an omelette made out of the long-eared owl's eggs was considered to be a remedy for drunkenness.

During the breeding season, the short-eared owl can mostly be found on open moorland in the uplands, from Orkney in the north, via the Western Isles, Scottish Highlands, northern England, and the Isle of Man, to further south, in parts of Wales and Staffordshire. Unusually for British owls, which are generally sedentary, it appears to be nomadic, breeding in large numbers in a particular habitat in some years, absent in others.

Short-eared owls have one of the most spectacular courtship displays of any British bird. On a clear, bright, early spring day, the male rises up into the sky on stiff, regular wingbeats, uttering his soft, hooting call. When he is sure that the female is watching, he lowers his wings and plummets rapidly towards her on the ground, while clapping his wings together beneath his body. Once seen, this can never be forgotten.

As soon as the pair-bond is fully formed, the female makes her nest (she is the only British owl actually to do so) by placing a few twigs into a shallow scrape among ground vegetation such as heather or bracken. Here she lays between four and seven white eggs, carefully concealed so that they – and the chicks, once they hatch – will not be easily seen by predators. While she undertakes the long and tedious duties of incubation, the male brings back food for her twice a day, usually in the early morning and early evening; he either drops the prey directly onto the nest, or she flies up to receive it in mid-air in what is known as a 'food-pass'.

After between twenty-four and twenty-nine days, the young hatch; soon afterwards, both male and female will head off to find food for them. Short-eared owls mostly prey on small mammals such as voles, rats and mice, which they hunt in the thick, dense moorland grass, but also take the occasional small bird or insect. After the breeding season is over, adults and youngsters will usually head south, to spend the autumn and winter months on coastal estuaries, freshwater marshes and rough areas of grassland or farmland. They do not seem to live as long as other owls: the oldest ringed bird was just six years and seven months old, whereas the oldest long-eared owl recorded, in Canada, lived almost twice as long, to twelve years old.

When I was growing up, in the suburbs to the west of London, I occasionally came across short-eared owls hunting on grassy areas around gravel pits, or on other areas of rough ground, but over the years the numbers dwindled, and I doubt if they would be found there today. I also regularly saw them on visits to the North Kent Marshes and North Norfolk; again, they are not so common there now.

Short-eared owls have declined on their once-regular wintering sites in my adopted county of Somerset, too. I have come across one here perhaps half-a-dozen times in the past couple of decades. The most memorable sighting was on a snowy Christmas Eve, back in 2010, while I was walking down the lane behind my home, with my brother-in-law Luke, his two dogs and my then five-year-old son George. We were just considering heading back to the warmth of home, when we noticed a brief movement in the hawthorn hedgerow alongside the road. Moments later, a short-eared owl emerged, heading away across the snow-covered field before landing on a distant gate and staring crossly back at us, before flying away high to the east. This was literally the only living wild creature we saw that day.

My yuletide encounter chimes with the Victorian ornithologist William MacGillivray, who wrote a useful account of the winter habits of the short-eared owl (which he dubbed the 'Streaked Tufted-owl') from his observations in eastern Scotland:

> It is found in stubble fields, or among turnips, by the side of a hedge, or on the grassy margin of a brook or ditch, where it rests in an erect posture. On being disturbed, it flies off in an undulating manner, with a buoyant flight . . . much in the manner of the smaller gulls.

His fellow-ornithologist George Montagu also carefully observed the behaviour of short-eared owls overwintering on his home patch near Kingsbridge in South Devon, noting that the bird is never seen perching in a tree, but instead 'generally hides itself in long grass, fern, or the like, and seems partial to open, barren situations. When disturbed it flies a little way, and lights again on the ground.'

I am not the only person seeing short-eared owls less often than I used to. With a recent estimate of only 1,400 breeding pairs in Britain, the species is threatened by disturbance and loss of habitat, and with both range and numbers having declined by as much as 50 per cent in recent years, the short-eared owl is now on the Amber List of Birds of Conservation Concern.

Recently the BTO launched a tracking project, using state-of-the-art GPS devices, to monitor the lives and travels of individual short-eared owls, in order to best work out their requirements, and improve the quality of their breeding habitats. This has produced some unusual and unexpected results: one female, tagged in Stirlingshire in 2017, first wandered widely around Scotland. Then, after breeding there the following spring, she left her mate to look after the young and headed all the way across the North Sea to Norway, where she appears to have bred again in the same season.

Following these wanderings, she was followed as she travelled all the way south to Ireland, Cornwall and Norfolk, before heading back to Norway in spring 2019, sadly dying in a storm as she approached the Norwegian coast. Another female, tagged on Arran in spring 2019, flew south to Devon, then that autumn crossed the English Channel to France, a following wind allowing her to fly at an average speed of over 82 kilometres (over 50 miles) per hour. Eventually she headed further south, all the way to Morocco. Like other migratory birds, these long-distance travellers need to balance the risks and dangers of making long journeys, with the potential advantages of being able to exploit new food resources.

Short-eared, and to a lesser extent long-eared, owls are the only migratory *Asio* species, and indeed – with the exception of the rare and irruptive snowy – the only British owls that regularly migrate: both species regularly travel some distance between their breeding and wintering grounds, regularly crossing the North Sea from Scandinavia to Britain. In November 2022, a long-eared owl boarded a fishing trawler more than 100 miles off the north coast of Scotland, and was spotted by a crew member who saw the bird being attacked by gulls. The owl was taken into care and fed chopped steak, before being cared for by a falconry centre on the mainland.

George Montagu knew the species by various names, including 'Hawk Owl', 'Mouse Hawk' and 'Woodcock Owl', the latter name referring to its arrival from continental Europe in October, at roughly the same time as another regular winter visitor. 'The hawk owl comes to us in October, about the time the woodcock makes its appearance, and departs the same time as that bird in March; hence the name of woodcock owl.'

Back in the 1970s, I witnessed this autumnal arrival for myself. Looking out to sea from the nature reserve at Cley in North Norfolk, I saw what looked like a floppy-winged raptor offshore, heading straight towards me. As it came closer, and I could finally see details of its shape and plumage – the mottled wings, streaked breast and rounded face – I realised to my astonishment that it was a short-eared owl.

Exhausted after its epic journey across the sea, it flopped straight down onto the shingle beach, before eventually managing to propel itself back into the air and head slowly inland. A few springs later I watched another migratory short-eared owl, this time heading north, on a fine May day above the Backs in Cambridge, completely unnoticed by tourists, dons and students alike, as they lounged on the grass, chatting and drinking, by the River Cam.

The long-eared owl, in contrast to the short-eared's preferences for open country, mostly breeds – and indeed spends much of its life – in dense woods and forests, making it much harder to see during the breeding season. 'It inhabits deep, dark fir woods,' wrote the Edwardian nature writer Reginald Bosworth Smith,

> where the sound of the woodman's axe is rarely heard . . . By day, the long-eared owl remains perched on a branch close to the bole of a Scotch fir [Scots pine] or spruce, with its body tucked up so tightly against it that it looks exactly like a knot or excrescence on its surface.

The presence of long-eared owls is usually discovered either because of the adult male's distinctive call – a regular, repetitive *hoo-hoo-hoo-hoo*, in tone much softer and quieter than the better-known hooting of the male tawny owl – or, later in the season, from the loud, whistling call made continuously by the youngsters as they beg for food, often described as sounding like a squeaky gate. Male long-eared owls can be heard calling regularly on their territories from early January, and the sound has been perfectly described by the wildlife cameraman John Aitchison as being like 'someone blowing over the top of a bottle'.

They breed mostly in coniferous, mixed and broad-leaved woods and forests, often close to the woodland edge, with access to more open, grassland or heathland habitats where the birds hunt for rodents under cover of darkness. They may initially be located by their display flights in late winter and early spring, when the males do a circuit of their territory at dusk or dawn, clapping their wings beneath their body like their short-eared cousins. Finding their nests can be very difficult, so in East Anglia scientists have put up woven willow baskets for the birds to breed in, hoping that as a result they will be able to study the nesting birds more closely.

The long-eared owl's nocturnal habits do make it easier to avoid being harassed by predators, but if one is attacked, according to George Montagu, 'it will throw itself on its back, and make a vigorous defence with its claws, hissing and snapping with its bill'.

Unusually, long-eared owls nest neither in holes, like tawny, barn and little owls, nor (at least usually) on the ground, like short-eared, snowy and eagle owls. Instead they generally take over an old nest made of sticks – often that of a magpie, crow or woodpigeon, or even a sparrowhawk's or heron's nest, or an old squirrel drey. The female then lays three or four white eggs at two-day intervals, which she incubates for roughly four weeks. The young, which leave the nest before they fledge – usually at about twenty-three to twenty-four

LONG-EARED OWL ♂ ♀ ♀

days old – are, like other baby owls, dependent on their parents for food for up to two or three months afterwards (hence the loud sounds they make), although they fledge into adult plumage at four to five weeks old.

As a breeding bird, the long-eared owl is thinly, yet fairly widely, distributed across Britain, with the highest densities in coastal areas of eastern Scotland and England, and also in parts of northern England and the Midlands. It is the most widespread owl in Ireland, where it generally inhabits dense woodland, almost certainly because it does not have to compete with the more dominant tawny owl, which is not found there.

Surprisingly, perhaps, the latest UK estimate of 3,900 breeding pairs is almost three times higher than that of the short-eared owl, and with a steady, rather than declining, population they are on the Green List, so not currently regarded as being of Conservation Concern. This is in contrast to the species' parlous status in North America, where the long-eared has declined at a faster rate than any other owl, with numbers down by more than 90 per cent since the 1970s. So far, scientists have failed to discover why this species' recent fortunes should be so different on either side of the Atlantic.

That there are more long-eared owls in Britain than we might have thought doesn't make them any easier to see, of course. They are usually most active in the two or three hours after dusk and before dawn, so are rarely seen during the hours of daylight. Like other owls, they have a main diet of rodents – rats, mice and especially voles – and because the numbers of these small mammals rise and fall cyclically, so do populations of long-eared owls. To counter this, the species is more nomadic than most other owls, breeding in different areas each year. They also occasionally take small birds, even, on occasion, catching swallows and martins in flight.

In the *Guardian* Country Diary, Mark Cocker wrote of his admiration for long-eared owls' hunting skills, having managed to observe a pair of adults catching voles for their young in Derbyshire's Goyt Valley. He marvelled at the birds' extraordinary ability to pinpoint the presence of these tiny rodents, and then use what he described as their 'laser-like acuity of hearing and a flight mode softer than the warm breeze', along with their almost supernatural sight, to find and catch their prey. 'Yet none of this conveys the intensity of the sight beam, the way the bird . . . scans and probes the realm of light photons, recoils the head to flame-throw its vision deeper into a spot.'

If you don't have Mark Cocker's fieldcraft – and indeed writing – skills, by far your best chance of coming across this enigmatic and elusive owl is during the autumn and winter months, when one or more birds may be discovered at their daytime roost in thick scrub or bushes. These are often at regular and publicly known sites such as RSPB or Wildlife Trust reserves, where they can be safely viewed from a distance, to avoid disturbance. Even so, in the past both nesting and roosting long-eared owls have been disturbed, as in 2020, when two juveniles are reported to have died at a known breeding site in Derbyshire. Birders and photographers have tried to get closer than they should to the roost, with predictable consequences, so many sites are no longer publicised.

William MacGillivray reported an account from one of his many correspondents, a 'Mr Hepburn', about what he called the 'Long-tufted Owl' being disturbed during the daytime – but in this case not by curious people, but smaller birds:

> He seeks the friendly shelter of the hedgerow or neighbouring wood, where he hopes to remain in peace until night again throws her veil over nature. Vain are his hopes, for a prying wren has discovered the intruder, and sounds an alarm. The robin, the whitethroat, the chanter, and other birds hasten to the spot . . . They buffet him, peck at, and menace him on every side, while the Owl turns his eyes from party to party, evading their blows as well as he can. The uproar is now great, each bird in his mother-tongue venting execrations against the poor Owl . . . At length he takes wing, generally flies a short distance, often pursued by a chaffinch or two.

In mainland Europe, oddly, the birds seem to be far more tolerant of people. Back in 1999 I filmed a long-eared owl roost in the city of Groningen, in the far north of the Netherlands, with perhaps twenty or more birds visible, seemingly unaffected by the steady passage of pedestrians and cyclists close by. But this pales into insignificance compared with the extraordinary winter gathering in the town of Kikinda, in northern Serbia, 150 km north of the capital, Belgrade.

Here, in December 2009, no fewer than 734 long-eared owls were counted at their winter roost in the central square, just outside the main

Eastern Orthodox church. Since then, numbers haven't risen quite so high, but there are usually 500 to 600 birds there on a regular basis throughout the winter months. This is, by a long way, the biggest single gathering of long-eared owls – perhaps any owls – anywhere on the planet.

This extraordinary spectacle was discovered as recently as after the turn of the millennium, by a local ornithologist, Milan Ružić. Since then, Milan, along with colleagues and visiting birders, including the Urban Birder David Lindo, has worked tirelessly to convince local people, who until then would have been indifferent or even hostile towards owls, that the birds could be a productive source of ecotourism revenue. The owls do their bit, too: it has been calculated that each winter they eat up to half a million voles and mice on the local farms.

It may seem puzzling that these usually shy birds should choose to roost in the middle of the town, rather than somewhere out of sight in the surrounding countryside. But it makes perfect sense: in Kikinda, the temperatures are generally a couple of degrees higher in rural areas, thanks to the 'urban heat island effect', while the constant glow of the streetlights deters most potential predators. David Lindo describes the scene awaiting visiting birders:

> The birds snooze during the day, wearily gazing down at their growing number of admirers . . . Just prior to dusk the birds become restless, sometimes sallying forth in a low floppy circular flight to land on a nearby tree or building. It is almost as though they were stretching their wings before the night's hunt in the outlying rural areas.

The international response to this unique gathering has been incredible. Thousands of visitors now travel here each year, many staying on to see Serbia's other sought-after bird species, bringing valuable revenue to other parts of the country. The media have come on board, too: as well as articles in *BBC Wildlife* magazine and the prestigious *Wall Street Journal*, the BBC Natural History Unit has filmed the scene for the landmark TV series *Planet Earth II*.

As David Lindo recalls, attitudes have dramatically changed since he first came to see the owls a decade or so ago:

> The locals looked at me as if I were a mad man when they saw me wandering around slack-jawed, gawping at the owls. Nowadays, a much warmer welcome awaits visiting birders. There are now shops open selling owl paraphernalia, and every November is now Owl Month, in which kids dress up as owls. Best of all, despite being an urban town square, the local government have made it a nature reserve – which is a world first . . . This is truly a fantastic conservation story that can only succeed if people continue to visit this remarkable square.

Globally, the long-eared owl can be found across the whole of the Holarctic region. In Europe and Asia, it breeds from Ireland and Iberia

in the west to China in the east, and from Scandinavia in the north to the Mediterranean and North Africa in the south; and in North America from British Columbia and Nova Scotia in the north, to California in the south. Birds in the northern part of their range, where the winters are too cold to stay put, migrate south during the autumn, wintering as far afield as Mexico and the Himalayan foothills.

Yet the long-eared owl's large range pales into insignificance compared with that of the short-eared owl. This is now (after the barn owl has been divided into three different species) by far the most widespread of all the world's owls, and indeed one of the most widespread of any landbird species.

The commonest of the short-eared owl's eleven different subspecies is found across much of Europe, North Africa, northern Asia and North America (where it is sometimes called the 'lesser horned owl' or 'cat owl'). Another widespread subspecies can be seen in southern South America as far south as Tierra del Fuego, while others have adapted to live on various Caribbean islands, Hawaii (to which it was probably brought by early explorers from Polynesia), northern South America, the Falkland Islands and even the Galápagos.

In parts of their range they have been reported as helping farmers and landowners, by helping to reduce plagues of rodents, as in this early-twentieth-century account by the US ornithologist Charles Wendell Townsend:

> When field mice or voles increase so as to become veritable plagues, various owls, especially of this species, have been known to congregate in the infested region and to have done great service in destroying the pests. There are several such records in various counties in England extending back to the sixteenth century.

A similar story, from the Canadian ornithologist Frank L. Farley, comes from central Alberta during the autumn and winter of 1931, when the stacks of wheat in the fields were infested with mice:

> The number of mice that this vast army of owls destroyed must have reached enormous proportions, and the birds may have prevented what

otherwise would have resulted in a serious plague. An invaluable service was rendered at a time of emergency, and at no cost whatever to the people.

Yet another example, if one were needed, of the value of owls to humans.

Short-eared owls do occasionally wander outside their usual range, sometimes causing serious problems for other species. A few years ago, a vagrant short-eared reached the mid-Atlantic archipelago of the Azores. Having arrived, it killed a substantial proportion of the local population of the rare and endangered Madeiran storm petrel, catching one or two birds each night, from a breeding colony of just 200 pairs. Others have wandered as far north as Spitzbergen, and as far south as Guinea-Bissau in West Africa, while one, fitted by scientists with a satellite transmitter, flew all the way from its Alaskan breeding grounds to spend the winter in Mexico, a journey of more than 7,000 kilometres.

The Galápagos subspecies of the short-eared owl, which is entirely confined to this remote Equatorial archipelago in the eastern Pacific Ocean, is noticeably smaller and darker than the ones we see in Britain and Europe or North America. It breeds on the ground, among lava rocks, in the higher areas of some of the more remote islands, and feeds mainly at dawn and dusk, or during the night. This is to avoid being attacked by the larger Galápagos hawk, the islands' main predator. However, on those islands where there are no hawks, the owls are able to hunt all day long.

As well as preying on baby marine iguanas, bats and lizards, and helping to keep down the populations of invasive mice and rats (which in turn will sometimes eat the owls' eggs), one of their main targets is the Galápagos petrel, a seabird endemic to the islands, which the owls catch by ambushing them as they emerge from their nesting tunnels below the rocky ground. They will even ambush the much larger blue-footed boobies, striking them on the back of their neck to kill them.

It's to be seen whether these unusual island races of the short-eared owl will eventually be separated into new species too, but they do show how, just like the barn owl, this adaptable species has learned to live in many different locations, habitats and climatic zones. As a result, it appears to be well insulated against the major environmental problems that currently threaten so many other owl species (see Chapter 9).

BRACHYOTUS PALUSTRIS.

R. 27.

7

SNOWY OWL

Owls in my culture have significant value when you see them. A lot of people fear the owl because most of the time it represents the death of a family member or somebody close to you . . . [But] it depends on how you look on it. For me it represented a death of something that I cherished and, for me, my message was that it is going to be OK.

Melissa Desmoulin (Pic River First Nation)

On a bright, cool and breezy day in June 1967, Bobby Tulloch was leading a visiting group of Swiss ornithologists across the hill of Stakkaberg, on the northern side of the island of Fetlar, in Britain's northernmost archipelago, the Shetland Isles.

As they tramped across the rough terrain, among the heather, sheep and Shetland ponies, Bobby was keeping a close eye on the rocky slopes, their boulders blanketed with moss and lichen. As well as some of Shetland's special breeding birds, such as whimbrel, golden plover and red-necked phalarope, he was also hoping to see a very rare visitor from the Arctic.

Eventually, Bobby glimpsed a movement, and a flash of white showing up against the grey-green landscape. It was a handsome male snowy owl – one of two males and a female that had been present on the island for over a year – taking flight a short distance ahead. He pointed out the bird to the group, and they all had good views, but something about the way it was behaving made him suspicious.

A few years later, when he was interviewed on BBC Radio Four's *Living World*, Bobby recalled what happened next:

Normally, during the daytime, they just sit huddled up in the lee of a rock, looking a bit fed-up. This one was sat on top of a rock, and looked a bit aggressive – it was glaring at us – and I thought perhaps it had been disturbed at a meal; perhaps it had caught a rabbit and was eating it. But something wasn't quite right, and I decided to look a bit more closely.

If Bobby's suspicions were correct, then it was crucial the group did not disturb the bird. So, telling the others to wait, he explained that he would head up the hill alone, on the pretext that he might find one of the bird's regurgitated pellets, and discover what it had been eating.

Then, just as he started to move closer, he saw another brief movement, and another tell-tale flash of white: this time a female snowy owl, which flew out from behind the rock. Now he faced a dilemma: should he retreat, and return later, to see if his suspicions were confirmed, or press on? Curiosity won, and he went a little further up the hill. Then he made the discovery that would change his life. 'To my amazement, there – on the ground, on a little ledge – were three large white eggs.'

Bobby knew he could not tell the party of ornithologists, who were watching him from just a hundred yards away. 'Much as I would have liked to have shouted it from the top of the hill, I didn't dare.' So he and the group headed back, the others blissfully unaware of his momentous discovery.

During his lifetime as a naturalist on his native Shetland, where for many years he was the RSPB's official representative, Bobby Tulloch had seen some remarkable sights. But finding the very first snowy owl's nest in Britain trumped them all. In the close-knit worlds of birdwatching, ornithology and conservation, the discovery would make this quiet, modest man into something of a celebrity; as it did, of course, the snowy owls themselves.

This may have been the first confirmed breeding record anywhere in the United Kingdom, but these striking visitors from the Arctic had been a scarce but mostly annual visitor to Shetland for over 150 years, becoming ever more regular from the early 1960s onwards.

The very first snowy owl recorded in Britain – an adult male – had been shot on the most northerly Shetland island, Unst, during the spring of 1812. This bird was 'collected' (to use the usual euphemism for killed) by Laurence Edmonston, a medical doctor from the islands' main town, Lerwick, who had first come across the bird there a year earlier, but had hitherto failed to get close enough to shoot it. Dr Edmonston presented this valuable and historic specimen to the celebrated naturalist and collector William Bullock. Consequently, in the summer of that year, Bullock decided to make the long and arduous journey north from his home in London to Orkney and Shetland, to try to see these special birds for himself.

When he arrived on the Orkney island of North Ronaldsay, he was informed that a white bird as large as a goose, with a head that resembled that of a cat, had been present for at least a month. He wasted no time in heading for the place where it had last been seen, a grassy rabbit warren close by the shoreline. Sure enough, the owl – another male – was there.

He managed to approach to within just 40 yards before it took flight. He quickly fired his gun, but missed, and the owl flew off.

Keen to obtain such a prize for his collection, Bullock then offered a handsome reward for anyone who could shoot it, following which various inexpert local marksmen took potshots at the owl, until it finally flew off to a neighbouring island, where it appears to have survived.

Subsequently, in *A History of British Birds*, Thomas Bewick noted that 'On his tour to the Orkney and Zetland [Shetland] isles, in the month of July, 1812, [Bullock] discovered that these birds breed there, and live chiefly upon rabbits, the Alpine hare, the Ptarmigan, and other birds.' Bullock's claim that the birds were breeding on Shetland was repeated by William Yarrell in his own three-volume *A History of British Birds*, published in 1843: 'They are seen there at the end of the summer, in company with their young, three or four together . . .' But his contemporary, the more rigorous and demanding William MacGillivray, disagreed: 'I have always doubted whether it bred here. Presumptions were in favour of the affirmative, but actual proof was wanting.' In MacGillivray's view, the presence of young in late summer did not prove that they had bred there; the birds could just as easily have travelled to Shetland as a family, from somewhere further north.

A century later, *The Handbook of British Birds* (the definitive mid-twentieth-century ornithological work) made no reference to snowy owls ever having bred – or even attempted to breed – in Britain. Whether, some time long before Bobby Tulloch's famous discovery, snowy owls really did nest undiscovered on one of the remote northern isles, we shall never know. But now, at last, they had.

When Bobby Tulloch found the snowy owls breeding on Fetlar, he immediately realised that they needed to be protected. In those days egg-collectors stealing the clutch was still a real problem – as was the possibility of a marksman shooting the adult birds. Local crofters were already reporting that the owls were behaving in an unusually aggressive manner towards them, so, as Bobby surmised, it was only a matter of time before people would put two and two together, and word would get out.

As a result, he and the RSPB immediately organised a round-the-clock guard on the nest. This worked: out of seven eggs that were originally laid, at two-day intervals from one another over almost a fortnight, the pair successfully hatched six young, of which five managed to survive to fledging.

For the next eight years, snowy owls bred every summer on Fetlar, raising young in every season but one. Overall, out of a total of forty-four eggs laid from 1967 to 1975, twenty-three (just over half) of the chicks fledged, although three of these did die soon afterwards.

From 1967 to 1972, the same pair of snowy owls bred every year. But in 1973, a second female – almost certainly one of the offspring from previous seasons – also took up territory, on the other side of the ridge from the first nest. The resident male bird immediately courted and mated with her, as well as with his original female, following which both laid clutches of eggs.

However, for the male, as Bobby Tulloch wryly recalled, 'when it came to feeding two families, the novelty soon wore off.' He deserted his second mate, forcing her to leave the nest at regular intervals to find food. This of course meant her eggs were very vulnerable and, sure enough, they were eaten by hooded crows.

The same pattern occurred the following year, 1974, while in 1975, the second female paired up with the male at the main nest, and the pair managed to raise four chicks: the most successful breeding attempt since the very first, eight years earlier.

That, however, was the very last time snowy owls bred here: not just on Fetlar or Shetland, but anywhere in Britain. The original male disappeared – having probably died – during the winter of 1975–76; and although one female, and sometimes two, remained on the islands into the early 1990s – even occasionally laying unfertilised eggs – no other males turned up, and they eventually left.

I visited Shetland for the first time in the summer of 1982, just after I left university. The fourteen-hour overnight boat journey from Aberdeen to Lerwick made me realise just how far north these islands are: closer, indeed, to Bergen in Norway than they are to Aberdeen; less than 6 degrees south of the Arctic Circle; as far from my childhood home in London as Prague, Milan or Barcelona.

The two days I spent on the island of Fetlar were among the most memorable of my entire birding life. I'll never forget walking across the marshy landscape one evening, when a tiny wader – which I eventually realised was a red-necked phalarope – flew up and circled around my head, uttering its delicate, piping call. The next morning, I stumbled across the phalarope breeding colony, before rapidly retreating a safe distance to avoid disturbing them. On a nearby loch, the brighter females, which in a reversal of normal bird behaviour take the lead in courtship, and have a burnt orange neck patch compared with the paler orange of the males, spun around for food in the shallow waters. They were so close that I could almost touch them.

But even that extraordinary experience was surpassed by the sight of a huge white bird sitting unobtrusively beside a lichen-covered rock, a couple of hundred metres away. It was a female snowy owl – my first, and still the only one I have seen anywhere in the world – staring straight back at me with her fierce black and bright yellow eyes.

SNOWY OWL
Nyctea scandiaca (*Linn*)

Scandinavian Nightbird. Ghost Owl. Ermine Owl. Tundra Ghost and – my favourite – the White Terror of the North. Just some of the numerous folk-names for 'a bird like no other', as Eugene Potapov and Richard Sale, authors of the definitive monograph on the snowy owl, put it.

It is, they go on, 'both a typical and atypical owl': cryptic – like all owls – yet conspicuous – like very few. It looks as if it must have evolved in the Arctic regions, yet it did not; while it remains mysterious, it has been known to the peoples who share its northerly home for millennia.

As both the folk names and the species' official name suggest, the breeding range of the snowy owl is the most northerly of all the

200-plus members of its family. It is native to the Holarctic – found mainly in the Arctic regions of North America, Europe and Asia – where it nests on open, bare tundra, and feeds mainly (at least during the breeding season) on lemmings.

For a long time, the species was placed in its own unique genus, *Nyctea*, but recent analysis of owl DNA has revealed that its closest relatives are actually the horned owls of North and South America, in the genus *Bubo*. It appears to have diverged from its nearest relatives (the closest being the great horned owl) about four million years ago. So, its scientific name is now *Bubo scandiacus*, meaning 'of Scandinavia', despite the fact that the species can be found across the whole of the Arctic region.

Male snowy owls are the world's only genuinely white owl, becoming whiter with age; females have a snow-white face, but the crown and the rest of their plumage – their back, wings and breast – are heavily marked with black (sometimes dark brown) blotching and barring. Because of their white coloration, snowies are the most obvious and distinctive of all the world's owls; indeed, when clearly visible they have a good claim to be one of the easiest of all the world's birds to identify.

As with many other owls – and raptors in general – the female snowy owl is considerably larger than her mate. Typically, a male is between 52 and 64 cm long, with a wingspan of 116 to 166 cm, and weighs somewhere between 1.5 and 1.8 kg. Females are slightly longer (between 54 and 71 cm, with a wingspan of 146 to 183 cm), but are considerably heavier, weighing up to 2.4 kg. They are one of the largest owls in the world: shorter in length, but noticeably heavier than another Arctic species, the great grey owl, and beaten overall for size only by some of the eagle owls, including the biggest of all, Blakiston's fish owl, found in Russia, China and Japan (see Chapter 9). Snowy owls are fairly long-lived: once they reach full adulthood, they typically survive for ten years, although some ringed birds have reached over twenty years of age.

As one of the region's most prominent birds, snowy owls have a special place in the mythologies and legends of the Arctic peoples. One Inuit legend – involving another much-mythologised bird – tells that a snowy owl and a raven were making new sets of clothes for one another, the raven making a white and black dress, the owl making a pure white one for the raven. But when the raven tried the dress on, it became so excited that the owl threw a pot of black paint over it, which is why ravens have been black ever since.

SNOWY OWL # 1

Ookpik, which means 'snowy owl' or 'Arctic owl' in Inuktitut, is also the name of one of the most popular of Inuit handicrafts, a souvenir sealskin owl with a large head and big eyes.

The First Nations of North America frequently feature snowy owls in their stories, viewing them as messengers from the dead, while much further south, the soul of a sinner who had repented was believed to fly to heaven in the form of a snowy owl. In a modern twist, one website listing '20 Signs that Winter will Suck in Michigan' included sightings of a snowy owl. But of all the cultural associations with the snowy owl, by far the best-known – albeit entirely fictional – individual is Hedwig, from J. K. Rowling's Harry Potter books and films.

Hedwig makes its appearance in the very first book of the series, *Harry Potter and the Philosopher's Stone*, published in 1997. It is bought by Professor Rubeus Hagrid, the Keeper of Keys and Grounds at Hogwarts, as a present for Harry's eleventh birthday. Hagrid (played in the subsequent film series by the Scottish actor and comedian, the late Robbie Coltrane) tells Harry he has chosen the owl specifically for its useful ability to carry messages: yet another nod to the durable fallacy that owls are especially intelligent. In fact, Harry would have been better off with a homing pigeon.

When the films of the books began to appear, from 2001, there was some concern that their popularity – and the undoubtedly impressive appearance of Hedwig itself – might lead to a rise in the illegal trade in owls as pets, similar to the massive rise in the keeping of terrapins as a result of the Teenage Mutant Ninja Turtles cartoons of the 1980s. Fortunately, studies later showed little or no correlation between the Harry Potter phenomenon and the keeping of owls, of any species, as pets.

Incidentally, although in the films Hedwig is referred to as female, 'she' is actually played by a series of all-white males – because, being smaller and lighter than the females, the male snowy owls were easier for the young actors to handle. Even so, Daniel Radcliffe, the actor playing Harry, had to wear a thick glove and a leather sleeve on his arm to protect him from the owl's sharp talons.

According to the account of the first nest on Fetlar, written by Bobby Tulloch for the journal *British Birds*, the snowy owls sensibly chose to breed on the north side of Stakkaberg, well out of sight of any nearby roads or habitation. The nest itself was a shallow scrape on a small patch of grass (to which a few dead tufts had been added by the adults), on a sloping slab of rock. This gave the female good views in most directions around the nest; anywhere she could not easily see could be observed by the male, from one of his look-out posts on the nearby rocks.

Bobby had discovered the nest very early on, during the first week of June, just a few days after the first egg had been laid. On their Arctic breeding grounds, snowy owls usually start laying their eggs by mid-May, and complete the clutch by the end of the month; making the Fetlar birds later than expected, especially given their more southerly latitude than the majority of the population.

When the chicks started to hatch, from the first week of July onwards, they emerged from the egg almost totally helpless, although still able to utter a faint cheeping. But during the following three weeks or so they grew very rapidly, and began to look less like little balls of fluff and more like actual owls.

Around that time, the older, larger chicks started to leave the nest, and by the time the eldest was four weeks old, they had all departed. Bobby recalled that the moss- and lichen-covered rocks around the nest provided perfect camouflage, making the chicks very hard to find; sometimes they would huddle together for security as they waited for one of the adults to return with food.

The parent owls were ruthlessly protective of their young, chasing off any other birds that dared to fly anywhere nearby, including predatory hooded crows, great-black-backed gulls and great skuas – known in Shetland as 'bonxies' – which could easily snatch an unwary chick. Conversely, the adult owls were often mobbed by other birds fearing for the safety of their own young. The adult snowy owls would react strongly to any human intruders into their territory, becoming agitated, and uttering warning sounds, the male's deep call reminiscent of a dog's bark, with the female calling at a higher pitch, rather like a screeching cat.

The adults would catch some birds for food: mostly juvenile

oystercatchers and Arctic skuas, but also a few rock doves, common terns, skylarks and a variety of waders. Otherwise – in the complete absence of lemmings, their usual food in the Arctic – they mostly fed their young on rabbits. The adults enjoyed the same diet: once the female was seen catching and swallowing a rabbit whole. They mainly hunted by using a 'sit-and-watch' technique, and mostly during the period Shetlanders call 'the simmer dim', between 10 p.m. and 3 a.m. when, because of the islands' northerly latitude, it never really gets dark.

In 1970, however, the disease myxomatosis – which wreaked havoc with rabbit populations – was introduced to Shetland. Within a year, rabbits had virtually disappeared from the islands, and the owls were temporarily forced to switch their diet to birds. This put Bobby and his colleagues in a quandary, as their target prey included some of Britain's rarest breeding waders, such as the whimbrel and red-necked phalarope. Fortunately, the rabbit population crash was only temporary; by 1974, numbers had more or less recovered, and they were once again the owls' main source of food for their chicks.

With so many people wanting to see the breeding snowy owls, the RSPB eventually erected an observation hut, which visitors could enter and leave without the birds noticing. For Bobby, however, the hide was too far away to get close-up photographs of the birds; so, to get close enough, in a tale he would tell to much amusement for many years afterwards, he and local photographer Dennis Coutts dressed up in the costume of a pantomime horse.

Dennis's photographs, and the careful and thorough observations made by Bobby Tulloch and his colleagues, are some of the most detailed ever made of a single nest of snowy owls. However, they may not be typical, as Fetlar lies at just over 60 degrees north, well towards the southern border of their usual range, which is mostly within, or close to, the Arctic Circle.

In the High Arctic, they return north to nest from April and May onwards. This is to take advantage of the very brief summer period of 24-hour daylight and abundant supplies of food, which usually allows them to raise a single brood of chicks each year. The further north they nest, the shorter the window available to lay their eggs and raise their young; they also need to time their arrival to coincide with the greatest abundance of lemmings, their most important food resource.

Having finished breeding – whether or not they have successfully raised any young to the fledging stage – snowy owls then begin to disperse. During the autumn they wander vast distances: each individual can cover as much as 2,900 km in a single season. They travel almost as far in late winter, in search of suitable places to nest. It has been calculated that the total winter range of a single snowy owl might cover as much as 364,000 square kilometres – roughly one-and-a-half times the total land area of the United Kingdom – and, coincidentally, about the same range as another iconic Arctic creature, the polar bear.

In autumn, unlike most species that nest so far north, snowy owls do not follow regular migration routes south. Instead they are what is known as partial (or irregular) migrants, with a large and complex winter range. The bigger adult females usually spend the winter further north than the smaller males, while first-year birds of both sexes head further south than both. They regularly reach the plains of Siberia, Mongolia and Canada, while others cross the border into the northern states of the USA, notably Minnesota. They have even been seen perching on blocks of sea ice, buoys and marine markers many miles offshore, where they hunt for sea ducks and other marine birds.

Like some other northern species such as the Bohemian waxwing (named after its wandering habits), snowy owls are irruptive, meaning that in some years they can turn up in unexpected locations, occasionally in unusually large numbers. As with other irruptive species, these movements usually occur after a productive breeding season; in North America, they happen on average once every three years.

Irruptive snowy owls have been seen as far south as Kentucky, Georgia, South Carolina and Florida in the east, and Utah, Colorado, Nevada and Texas in the west. They have even occasionally reached the archipelagos of Bermuda and Hawaii, which are, respectively, at the same southerly latitudes as Morocco and central Mexico. During the winters of 2011–12 and 2014–15, record counts of snowy owls – almost all juvenile birds – occurred in parts of Canada and the United States, including places where the species is usually very rare.

Some southbound snowy owls have even been found hitching a ride on fishing vessels travelling from the Arctic: in October 2001, a

group of twelve owls boarded a ship off Quebec in Canada and hitch-hiked all the way to Europe, periodically disembarking once the ship was within reach of land, off the coasts of Scotland, Belgium, the Netherlands and the UK. Several were exhausted after their long journey, and so were taken into captivity, with seven Dutch birds ultimately being released further north, on suitable breeding grounds in Finland.

More than a century earlier, in February 1886, the crew of the steamship *Ulunda* were astonished to see a snowy owl landing on the rigging of their ship, more than 800 kilometres from the nearest land. The bird was captured and taken by the ship's captain to his eventual destination in London. There it was stuffed and mounted, and sent to the Maritime Museum in Halifax, Nova Scotia, where it can still be seen today.

In January 2021, a female snowy owl turned up unexpectedly in New York's Central Park – the first one recorded in Manhattan for over 130 years, since 1890. It had apparently mistaken the park's prominent base-ball diamond for a beach, and was regularly and persistently harassed by the resident crows and red-tailed hawks, clearly confused and dis-concerted by this huge white stranger in their midst.

Not surprisingly the bird became a media celebrity, attracting many hundreds of excited birdwatchers, one of whom described seeing the owl as 'like winning the lottery'. 'The hordes came running,' reported the *New York Times*,

cameras and spotting scopes in hand, and the snow-white raptor with the thick black bars that mark a young female was the latest instant-celebrity bird of Manhattan – a sequel to both Rocky the Rockefeller Center Christmas tree owl from last year and the superstar mandarin duck that ruled the park and the world's social-media feeds in 2018.

Soon, however, the crowds, noise and attention became too much for this usually solitary bird, and the following day she disappeared, not to be seen again. For disappointed latecomers, the *New York Times* offered an alternative experience: a stuffed and mounted snowy owl, on display in the nearby American Museum of Natural History. This bird had been shot on nearby Long Island during the winter of 1876, by none other than a teenage Theodore (Teddy) Roosevelt, future 26th President of the United States and, ironically, one of the world's first conservationists.

Back in Britain, following those early-nineteenth-century records, more snowy owls have turned up from time to time. There have been regular sightings from St Kilda, the Cairngorms and the Western Isles, and in January 2018, one reached as far south as the Isles of Scilly. For several summers during the 1980s and 1990s, the Cairngorms played host to both males and females, but sadly any hopes that they might pair up and breed came to nothing. In 2001, a pair did breed unsuccessfully in the Irish county of Donegal; two years earlier, in 1999, five 'white owls' (presumably an entire family) were seen in the west of the county, suggesting that snowy owls might possibly have bred there earlier that year.

There have been a surprising number of records further south, in Norfolk, following one shot in 1814 (the first British mainland record). In March 2018 a female was seen regularly at the RSPB reserves of Snettisham and Titchwell, following the brief but brutal spell of unseasonably cold weather dubbed by the tabloids 'the Beast from the East'. The owl was initially discovered at Snettisham by a puzzled passer-by, who then showed a photo taken on his phone to the reserve's volunteers. They soon tracked it down and confirmed its identity; fortunately, the bird stayed around for long enough to be seen by more than 800 delighted visitors.

Partly because of the snowy owl's wandering habits, and partly because it lives in some of the world's harshest and most inaccessible habitats, it is very difficult to work out how many individuals there are in the world, and whether that number is rising or falling. The species has now been listed as 'Vulnerable' by BirdLife International, mainly because of recent rapid declines in North America, and possible falls in numbers in Scandinavia and Russia. The latest estimate is of a global population somewhere between 14,000 and 28,000 birds, spread over a huge area, of perhaps 38 million square kilometres – more than the land area of Russia, the United States and Canada put together. Should numbers continue to fall, the snowy owl might soon be moved into the 'Endangered' category.

So why is this species in so much trouble? Being such low-flying birds, and covering such large distances across the Arctic landscape, snowy owls are especially susceptible to collisions with aircraft, vehicles, buildings and structures such as energy pylons and cables. In winter, the birds often hunt for food around airfields and airports, which increases the risk of bird strikes, for both the birds and the passengers and crew. So far, thankfully, no humans have lost their lives owing to collisions with snowy owls, but it can surely only be a matter of time.

In one study, of 438 banded (ringed) snowy owls that had been found dead, virtually all known causes of death involved humans. These included birds that had been shot, trapped, hit by road vehicles or aircraft, or accidentally collided with towers or wires. In north Norway, snowies are often disturbed near their nests by dogs, birdwatchers, scientists, tourists and reindeer herders. Although they are no longer killed in the numbers they used to be – sometimes the hundreds – by hunters, or by indigenous people for food, it is still legal for Arctic communities to hunt them.

As with so many of the world's vulnerable species of bird, the climate crisis is by far the greatest danger to its long-term survival. Temperatures are rising in the polar regions at a much faster rate than anywhere else on the planet, bringing a greater likelihood of parasites and diseases, a reduction of sea ice, and even a risk of hyperthermia – overheating – caused when these heavily feathered birds warm up too quickly. The warming climate is also encouraging more commercial exploitation of natural resources in the area, leading to further conflict with the owls.

Rapid rises in temperature are also having a negative impact on the snowy owl's main prey species: lemmings. In Greenland, lemming numbers have fallen from an average of twelve per hectare to just two, leading to a 98 per cent drop in breeding success for the region's snowy owls. Ultimately, even with just a 1.5-degree Celsius rise in global temperatures (the current target), the suitable habitat for this majestic bird in North America is predicted to fall by over half. Snowy owls are tough birds – they have to be, to live where they do – but they are unlikely to be able to cope with such a lethal combination of threats and problems.

Ironically, perhaps, the main reason snowy owls bred in Britain at all, back in the late 1960s and early 1970s, was that this period coincided with a brief spell of 'climatic cooling', following a slow but definite reduction in global average temperatures since the 1940s. This was especially noticeable in north-west and northern Europe, and led to a temporary extension in range of a number of Scandinavian species into Britain. Now that this very short-term trend has been reversed, and average temperatures in north-west Europe are rising rapidly, snowy owls are very unlikely ever to breed in Britain again.

Bobby Tulloch, the Shetlander who found fame (if not fortune) by discovering the very first British snowy owl nest, spent the remainder of his life happily showing his beloved whimbrels, golden plovers and red-necked phalaropes – though not, alas, the long-departed owls – to visitors from all over the world. In 1994, 'Mr Shetland', as he was known, was deservedly awarded the MBE for his long and dedicated services to ornithology and conservation.

In the summer of 1997, I took a film crew to Shetland, to film an episode for the second BBC-TV series of *Birding with Bill Oddie*. We had hoped to meet Bobby there and persuade him to tell, once again, the extraordinary tale about how he came across that precious clutch of snowy owl eggs more than thirty years earlier.

Sadly, we could not. Just over a year earlier, in May 1996, following a series of strokes, Bobby had died, at the age of just sixty-seven. The many obituaries focused, quite rightly, on the discovery of the owls. But there was also an outpouring of affection from the many hundreds of people who had had the pleasure and privilege of meeting him, as I had in the early 1990s, when I would come across Bobby at the annual British Birdwatching Fair, sitting quietly with another gentle, bearded RSPB pioneer, the late Bob Scott, and exchanging stories about the good old days.

$\frac{1}{4}$

Litho. W. Greve, Berlin.

EAGLE-OWL.

Bubo maximus, *Fleming.*

8

EAGLE OWL

The Bubo [Eagle Owl] is a fatal bird, of evil omen beyond other sorts . . . monster of the night, it utters not a song, but only a groan.

Pliny the Elder, *The Natural History* (AD 77)

That evening the young couple had just set out for the short walk across Ilkley Moor to their local pub, when they were viciously attacked. There was a strange, whirring noise behind them, and they turned round just in time to see a huge bird heading straight towards them out of the darkness.

'It was flapping wildly, its talons reaching for [my partner's] head,' the man remembered afterwards, 'but as she screamed and waved it realised it had made a mistake and swooped down to land about ten feet away. I couldn't help thinking, "My God, that's a big bird!"'

It was indeed. For this was no familiar little, barn or tawny owl, but a Eurasian eagle owl: not just the largest member of its family in Europe but the second biggest species of owl anywhere in the world. At up to 70 cm long, with a wingspan close to 2 m, and weighing between 2.3 and 3.3 kg, the eagle owl is a formidable adversary. With few natural enemies (apart of course from man), this is one of the key apex predators across much of Europe, even attacking and killing other large birds of prey.

The eagle owl is a magnificent and, given good views, unmistakable creature. It looks rather like a giant long-eared owl, with mottled black, brown and buff plumage, prominent ear tufts, and bright orange eyes. These, combined with the 'horns' on its head and loud, screaming call, have led to the species being dubbed 'the devil's helper' in parts of

Scandinavia. As the Norwegian ornithologist Edvard K. Barth wrote, 'The Eurasian eagle owl is the largest, most mythical, and most feared of all owls.'

So what was it doing in West Yorkshire?

'A full-scale capture operation is under way on Ilkley Moor,' reported the local newspaper, the *Telegraph and Argus*, 'after a massive European Eagle Owl terrorised walkers at the weekend.' Bradford Council's Countryside Service was mobilised, and action became more urgent when a second attack was reported, on a local firefighter and his six-year-old daughter. Previously, it turned out, the owl had also swooped down on several local dogs being walked across the moor.

'Owls that!' exclaimed the newspaper a few days later. 'The eagle [owl] has landed and been captured.' The bird – which had apparently been living in the area for two years – had been trapped and taken into captivity. Readers were left in little doubt that it did not belong in Yorkshire. It was described as 'native to northern European countries including Scandinavia', and the officer who had managed to catch the bird declared that this had been necessary 'for the sake of the moor's native wildlife', which apparently included rabbits.

The RSPB tentatively agreed, noting that 'more and more people are keeping large owls in captivity and we are concerned at the number escaping.' It also suggested that the owl had escaped or been deliberately released by a local falconer, which might explain why it had approached people in the first place, as it would associate humans with providing it with food. Another member of its team stated categorically that 'the bird is not native to Britain and its presence in the area was causing concern. It posed a threat to other bird populations and, just as worrying, carried the threat of attack to walkers on the moor.'

Intriguingly, though, the man who had been the victim of the initial attack later admitted to mixed feelings about it ending up in captivity. It was 'interesting to have in the area, and obviously surviving quite well in the wild'. Another woman, who had seen the bird perched on her balcony on the night it was captured, agreed.

I watched it through the window, just feet away from my face. It was a marvellous sight, very big with large green, beady eyes. I'm quite upset it has been caught, poor creature – I know it shouldn't attack people but I think it should be out and about and have its freedom.

The story of the Yorkshire eagle owl has a parallel in North America; this time in an urban setting: the heart of New York City. In early February 2023, a Eurasian eagle owl named Flaco (from a Spanish word meaning 'skinny') managed to escape from Central Park Zoo, after a hole had been cut in his cage by unknown vandals. Like the wild snowy owl that had briefly visited the park just two years earlier, Flaco soon became a huge celebrity, with crowds of birders – and curious members of the public – flocking there to catch sight of this enormous bird.

At first, there were concerns that he would not be able to catch food, and might starve to death; Flaco soon proved the doubters wrong, by making heavy inroads in to the park's large population of rats, leading some to suggest that he should be allowed to remain free. However, there were also very real fears that he might die from consuming rat poison from one of his victims, or be killed by traffic – a fate that befell another escaped eagle owl near Minnesota Zoo in 2021.

At the time of writing, Flaco has managed to avoid all attempts at capture, and remains at large. But Flaco is not the only large owl present in New York's city centre. A great horned owl nicknamed Geraldine – a genuinely wild bird, and the largest native owl species in the Americas – is also living nearby. Her territory is about a mile away from Flaco's, earning them the joint title of 'the King and Queen of Central Park'.

Great horned owls – which have yellow, not orange eyes – are not quite as big as Eurasian eagle owls, but are still a very large and impressive creature. Like Flaco, Geraldine has, perhaps not surprisingly, also become a social media star, with video clips and updated sightings regularly posted on Twitter and other platforms.

Unlike the rest of Europe (with the obvious exception of Ireland), Britain has not only lost almost all its big, fierce animals such as the bear, wolf and lynx; in doing so, we have also lost our once-profound connection with them.

As the original article about the Ilkley Moor owl noted, the Eurasian eagle owl – scientific name *Bubo bubo* – can be found across a wide swathe of Europe and Asia, from Portugal in the west, via virtually the whole of Russia and China, to Korea and Japan in the east; from the edge of the tree line in Norway and Finland in the north, to the Middle East and northern India in the south; and up to an altitude of almost 5,000 metres above sea level in the Himalayas and the Tibetan Plateau.

EAGLE OWL ♀ ♂

It is one of nineteen species in the genus *Bubo*, including the snowy, great horned, lesser horned and Blakiston's fish owls, along with several other species with 'eagle owl' in their name, found across much of tropical Asia and Africa.

Almost everywhere the Eurasian eagle owl lives, so do human beings, and, as with other major predators, people seem to be able to live alongside the species without resorting to hysterical headlines or calls for the birds to be removed from the wild. Of course, if the Ilkley Moor bird was originally an escapee, it was probably best that it was caught and returned to captivity. But there is some doubt whether all the many other eagle owls that have been reported in the wild in recent years are indeed non-native escapees, and so, to use an emotive word which resonates with human immigrants, 'aliens'.

The latest (2022) version of the official British Ornithologists' Union's 'British List', the comprehensive and authoritative checklist of all bird species recorded in a wild state in Britain, includes nine species of owl. They are the six species featured in this book's previous chapters (tawny, barn, little, long-eared, short-eared and snowy owls), plus three vagrants: Tengmalm's, scops and hawk owls. As this shows, the BOU does not consider the eagle owl to be an official British bird, but it does give the species a separate section on its website, accompanied by a painting of the bird by artist Richard Allen, which describes the status of the eagle owl in Britain as having 'had a chequered history. In recent years several key investigations have been undertaken looking at the fossil record and evidence of contemporary records.'

These are summarised in a 2008 paper in *British Birds*, published following a major rise in sightings of apparently wild eagle owls in various parts of Britain, with well-known pairs breeding in northern England, including one pair in the Forest of Bowland, Lancashire, and another in Northumberland. The authors' job was to try to discover the origin of these birds, in order to decide whether the eagle owl should be admitted to the British List, following its removal as recently as 1996. That had come after a thorough analysis of earlier records of the species – until then considered to be a scarce but occasional visitor to Britain – which deemed them either to be not fully documented, possible misidentifications of other large owls, or simply escapees from captivity.

As the paper pointed out, it is often very hard to judge the actual size of a lone bird, and on closer inspection many of the supposed sightings of 'eagle owls' from the Northern Isles (Orkney and Shetland) turned out to be short-eared or long-eared owls. The authors went on to analyse the likelihood that some – or indeed any – of the recent records of eagle owls in Britain might be wild birds. They looked at the owls' behaviour – for example, attacking humans who approached their nest, which is at odds with continental European birds, which are rarely aggressive to intruders. They also investigated the cage bird trade, revealing that an estimated total of 3,000 to 4,000 eagle owls are held in captivity in Britain – a phenomenally high figure – of which over 120 had been reported as lost, with more than seventy of these apparently never recaptured.

Finally, they examined the likelihood of wild eagle owls arriving naturally in Britain, after flying across the North Sea from continental Europe. After all, as we have seen, both short-eared and long-eared owls regularly migrate from Scandinavia to Britain, as have, on a few occasions, hawk and Tengmalm's owls. So why couldn't eagle owls?

Writing at the turn of the nineteenth century, Thomas Bewick had asserted that 'the bird is sometimes met with in the northern Scottish isles, where it preys upon Rabbits and Grouse . . . but it is very rarely seen in England.' Later, in the 1860s, James Harting was equally confident, writing of the occurrence of an apparently wild 'Great Horned

EAGLE OWL

Owl' (an alternative name for the species) in Hampstead, then just a quiet country village, rather than part of urban London:

> It was caught, after much trouble, in a hedge near the house, and was kept for some time until it died. It was very fierce during captivity, and had been severely wounded in its wing by shot, previously to its capture.

However, it appears both Bewick and Harting were wrong. Unlike short-eared and long-eared owls, which are known to be both migratory and nomadic in their behaviour, eagle owls are generally very sedentary; thus, as the authors of the 2008 paper conclude, they 'would be no more likely to turn up in Britain than would a Tawny Owl in Ireland'.

Neither have any eagle owls been recovered from oil and gas

platforms in the North Sea, a regular stopping point and resting place for the two 'eared' species. And finally, ringing data from Scandinavia suggests that eagle owls very rarely fly over even narrow areas of water, with not a single record of a ringed bird crossing the 20 km of sea that separates Sweden from Denmark. As they conclude, 'The BOU must have a very strong case for adding any species to the British List . . . Currently, the known records do not meet [the] criteria.'

Yet another organisation, the BTO, remains unsure, its 'BirdFacts' page on the eagle owl categorising the species rather tentatively as an 'Escaped (?) Breeder', and describing it as 'commonly kept in captivity, but following a first breeding attempt in Morayshire, 1–2 pairs have bred every year since 1996, notably in Yorkshire; they may yet establish themselves as part of our bird fauna.'

But even if most, perhaps all, of the recent records of eagle owl might be of birds accidentally or deliberately released into the British countryside, does that mean that the species should still be classified as 'non-native'? The ornithologist James Fisher did not believe so: he tentatively suggested that eagle owls were 'possibly native [from the] eighth to the eleventh centuries'.

We do know that eagle owls lived in Britain, alongside other apex predators and early humans, during prehistoric times. In her 2021 book *Beak, Tooth and Claw: Living with Predators in Britain*, the conservationist Mary Colwell paints a vivid and detailed picture of Kents Cavern, now a popular tourist site near Torquay in Devon. Here, packs of wolves, wild horses and cattle, and even rhinos and mammoths, would have roamed the land, being hunted by – and sometimes hunting and killing – the early humans living in caves. Mary also describes large birds of prey 'sailing in the sky, looking down on the battles below', whose bones have been found in the caves. And along with the species we might expect – white-tailed and golden eagles, kites and buzzards,

Eagle owls hunted birds and often nested in caves. Their soft, lonely hoots would have floated across the hard ground, a remarkably gentle sound for a bird whose wingspan is nearly 2 metres.

Despite the lack of evidence that even one wild eagle owl has ever managed to make it to our shores under its own steam in recent times, in the last paragraph of the *British Birds* paper, the authors suggest one further route to acceptance as an official British bird: via 'Category C' of the British List. This category includes species that originally escaped into the wild in Britain, rather than arriving naturally – for example, the Canada goose, rose-ringed parakeet and mandarin duck. If a species manages to form a self-sustaining breeding population – rather than escaped birds occasionally breeding – then it can, after a period of time, be admitted to the list.

In November 2005, a BBC-TV programme, *Natural World: Return of the Eagle Owl*, showed footage of a family of eagle owls on Ministry of Defence land on the North York Moors. It turned out that this pair had been present for almost a decade, during which time they had reared no fewer than twenty-three offspring. Once the young owls fledged, only one bird had been rediscovered, more than 130 miles from where

it was born, having collided with a power line in Shropshire and been electrocuted. Although eagle owls can live up to twenty years in the wild, the leading cause of death is electrocution – the bird has such a large wingspan that unfortunately it sometimes touches both power lines when taking off.

Soon after the programme was broadcast, the female of the Yorkshire pair was herself killed: shot by someone who would clearly prefer that the species did not get a toehold in the British countryside. The Cumbria-based charity the World Owl Trust condemned the killing as 'disgraceful', and called for the species to be added to the British List – which would automatically give it legal protection – but when it comes to the species' presence in Britain the Game and Wildlife Conservation Trust, the RSPB and even many birders and conservationists have remained on the fence.

Other commentators, including the environmental historians Professor Ian Rotherham and Dr Rob Lambert, take a more relaxed view. They criticise the appearance of the species on an official list of 'non-native species that pose a threat to Britain's indigenous animals' under the Wildlife and Countryside Act of 1981. As they point out, given the long history of eagle owls in Britain (longer than the history of modern humans here), lumping this species and other former natives into the same category as genuinely invasive, non-native species like the grey squirrel, is a worrying development, as it shows a total misunderstanding of the difference between a non-native and destructive species and one that did once live here in Britain.

They also muse on the economic advantages of 'eagle owl tourism': attracting birders and photographers, and thus boosting rural economies, in the same way that 'sea eagle tourism' has become such a success on the Isle of Mull (and more recently the Isle of Wight).

Nevertheless, in 2010, a government risk assessment concluded that a rising population of eagle owls in Britain could pose 'a significant threat' to other predators, including hen harriers. Given that this elegant raptor faces the constant and very real threat of illegal killing by landowners and gamekeepers, to protect their precious grouse, the presence of a few eagle owls is hardly significant.

The veteran conservationist Roy Dennis, who during the past six decades has done more than anyone to bring back former native species, including the osprey, red kite and white-tailed eagle, is an enthusiastic supporter of eagle owls, which he believes were hunted to extinction in Britain some time in the distant past, regarding them as an essential top predator which, having been lost, diminishes our nation's biodiversity. The BBC programme's producer, Fergus Beeley, agrees:

> Like it or not, eagle owls are here and more are bound to arrive as numbers grow in Europe. As predators of predators they may take some of our more familiar wildlife, but perhaps that's a small price to pay for sharing our land with such a magnificent wild creature.

Whether the Eurasian eagle owl will become part of our native avifauna, and eventually accepted as a true British bird – even by default – is very much in the balance. What nobody can doubt is that this is one of the most impressive and charismatic owls on the planet.

9

OWLS AROUND THE WORLD

Where the bee sucks, there suck I,
In a cowslip's bell I lie,
There I couch when owls do cry.

William Shakespeare, *The Tempest*,
Act V Scene I (1611)

During the past thirty years and more, as a birder, author and wildlife television producer with the BBC Natural History Unit, I have been fortunate to travel to all six continents where owls can be found. They are, of course, often tricky to find and, even when you do come across them, can be very hard to identify. Sometimes all I have managed is a brief glimpse of a mysterious broad-winged creature melting into the darkness. But over time I have managed to see forty different species, encounters with some of which I share with you now. I shall then discuss the future for the world's owls, and in particular how we can help them survive in such challenging times.

The first owl I ever saw – apart from those species I had already come across in Britain – was a tiny little creature, barely the size of a starling. I was walking along a path at the vast wetland of Bharatpur, in northern India, on my very first birding trip abroad, in February 1985, when a spotted owlet appeared briefly close by – looking rather like an animated children's toy. My most recent new species, a southern white-faced owl, was in Manyoni Game Reserve, South Africa, in January 2020, on my last foreign trip before the pandemic struck. We had been on a night drive looking for Africa's most endangered mammal, the pangolin, and were returning to camp just before midnight when our guide spotted this charismatic owl perched in the lower branches of a tree, its pale white face shining back at us through the darkness.

Actually, I very nearly saw my first non-British owl at the age of eighteen, in the spring of 1979. I was staying on the Greek island of Santorini, during my gap year. One evening, walking back to our camp-site after dark, my friend Rob and I heard a bizarre sound coming from the top of a telegraph pole in the village street, just a few feet above our heads. It was a regular bleeping, uttered every two or three seconds, which we eventually decided must be mechanical and man-made. Dec-ades later, when I finally heard the bizarre, repetitive call of a Eurasian scops owl – a metronomic *beep . . . beep . . . beep* – I finally realised that this was what I had heard all those years ago.

In between my first and last encounters with 'owl lifers', there have been many other highlights, some during filming trips with the BBC. These were usually when we were deliberately searching for a particu-lar species, but occasionally complete flukes, when we simply stumbled across an owl after dark.

Back in early 1989, when I worked for BBC Continuing Education, we were making a Spanish language series, *Mexico Vivo*, on the Yucatán Peninsula. After an exhausting day's travelling, we were relaxing by the hotel swimming pool on the island of Cozumel, drinking salted marga-ritas out of polystyrene cups, when suddenly, flying right above our heads, a smallish owl appeared. As it hovered, briefly illuminated by the swimming pool lights, I saw just enough detail – bright yellow eyes, two distinctive ear-tufts – to tentatively identify the bird as one of the screech owls. But this is a widespread group across the Americas, with more than twenty different species – so which one was this?

Fortunately, a US birding group was also staying at the hotel, and I mentioned my sighting to the leader. I have rarely seen a bird guide – even one from the United States – get so excited. 'Oh my God!!!

Vermiculated screech owl!!!!!" he yelled, much to the amusement of my non-birding colleagues. The next morning, I was delighted to discover that he and the group had stayed up until the owl had – fortunately – returned, and he was able to confirm the identification.

I saw another member of the same genus – the much commoner eastern screech owl – in autumn 1996, at Lake Kissimmee in Florida, when I was filming for the first series of *Birding with Bill Oddie*. We were playing a tape recording of its haunting, tremulous call – a series of repeated, trilling notes, sounding rather like a whinnying pony – to attract smaller songbirds for us to film.

Sure enough, as soon as the tape was turned on, they flocked frantically around us to mob what they assumed was an intruding owl. Then we got to see the bird itself, showing off its greyish-brown plumage and characteristic ear-tufts as it also came over to find out what on earth was going on, offering us surprisingly close and prolonged views. Since then I have seen bird guides use the same trick to attract another common and widespread species, ferruginous pygmy owl, in Trinidad and Costa Rica.

During the recce for that Florida filming trip, on a blisteringly hot day in late August, the cameraman, researcher and I turned up at Cape Coral, on the southern edge of the city of Fort Myers, to search for one of the world's most unusual owls. The burrowing owl does exactly what its name suggests: unlike most other owls, rather than nesting in holes in trees, buildings, or on cliff ledges, it breeds in burrows in the ground. It is mostly diurnal in its habits, as the Victorian nature writer Edward Stanley reported, using observations made by Napoleon Bonaparte's younger brother Lucien:

> This bird enjoys the broadest glare of the noon-day sun; searches for
> food during the cheerful light of the day; and then returns to its

underground dwelling, which consists of the burrows of the marmot, or prairie-dog.

These burrows, which, when suitable sites are not available, the birds dig for themselves, using their long, powerful legs, are sometimes taken over as hiding places by a very unwelcome intruder: rattlesnakes. But the crafty owls have managed to use this to their advantage: when they feel threatened by a coyote, domestic cat or dog, or indeed a different species of snake, they retreat inside their burrow and make a loud, rattling sound, just like that of a rattlesnake, which usually has the desired deterrent effect.

Fortunately, on the day we visited, there weren't any rattlesnakes around. Neither, however, were there any owls. We wondered if the midday heat was too much, even for this famously diurnal bird. And then, in the scrubby undergrowth around the burrow, we noticed a small movement.

Sure enough, moments later, our first burrowing owl appeared; popping up his head like a meerkat, then turning rapidly left and right to check for danger. Presumably deciding that we were not planning to do him any harm, he proceeded to stretch up on his long legs, and then ran across the grass in front of us, looking as if he were on stilts. We returned a couple of months later with Bill Oddie, and obtained some wonderful footage of these curious birds as they hopped around the entrance to their burrow, much to his, and my, delight.

I was again with Bill when, in April 2002, we both saw our first Eurasian pygmy owl – Europe's smallest species, barely the size of a sparrow – on a springtime visit to southern Sweden. A couple of decades later, I watched a female pygmy owl (larger than its mate, but still tiny), located by my friends Hania and Marek Borkowski in the forest near their home on Poland's Biebrza Marshes. On both occasions, I could not believe how something so small could be quite so feisty, like the avian equivalent of a bantamweight boxer.

On that same, memorable visit, Marek showed me my first Tengmalm's owl, a plump little bird with a dark brown plumage and pale face, briefly poking its head out from a nest hole in the Białowieża Forest, where we also witnessed a huge eagle owl flying straight over our heads at dusk, on long, broad wings. Finally, on an unforgettable day, he took me across the Belarus border, where, as well as coming across a huge herd of European bison, we watched a female great grey owl – Europe's second largest species after the eagle owl – tentatively raising her head up out of her nest to check us out. I had been hoping to see this bird for many years, and was struck by its rather bizarre appearance: two oddly tiny, yellow eyes, placed close together in the centre of her rounded head.

Some of the most unusual places I have ever seen owls are the Negev Desert and nearby Arava Valley, in southern Israel, both in the company of the man widely considered to be the world's leading field birder, Hadoram Shirihai. The first, the wonderfully named pharaoh eagle owl, was somewhere in the middle of the Negev; as ever, a frustratingly brief view after dark. Here, a few years later, I watched another, flying overhead in fading light, at the burial site and memorial for Israel's founder and first prime minister, David Ben-Gurion. Surprisingly small for an eagle owl, it then reappeared and chased off a passing fox, before perching back on the cliff face as dusk fell.

That same year I was back with Hadoram, together with the Irish bird artist Killian Mullarney, as we took a long hike up a side valley in the Arava Valley. We were in search of what was then called Hume's tawny owl, named after the pioneering nineteenth-century British ornithologist, Allan Octavian Hume. We searched the cliff face for what seemed like hours, as the night-time temperature began to plummet and I wished I had worn warmer clothes. Then, at last, Hadoram spotted it: looking rather like a pale grey version of our own familiar tawny owl, perched on a nearby cliff, staring back towards us with what I noted at the time was an 'astonished' appearance.

A few years later, it was my turn to be astonished, when it was announced that, owing to a mix-up in the classification of various kinds of owls found in the Middle East and Asia, this species would henceforth be renamed the 'desert owl'. It also gained a new scientific name, *Strix hadorami*, making Hadoram Shirihai one of the handful of living ornithologists to have had a species of bird named after him.

But perhaps the most extraordinary owl I have ever come across – against strong competition – was the bird I was taken to see in Botswana's Okavango Delta in December 2008, while on a recce for an ill-considered, and ultimately disastrous, wildlife reality TV show called *Wildest Dreams*.

That morning I had already done a river trip by *mokoro*, the wooden dugout canoes favoured by the delta's indigenous people, past groups of hippos eyeing us up with what looked like quietly murderous intent. So I was relieved when my quest, for one of the world's most charismatic and hard-to-see owls, turned out to be on foot.

We were walking through the open riverine forest near Wilderness Safaris' Vumbura Plains Camp, when my guide suddenly grabbed my arm and pointed urgently ahead. It was just in time for me to see a huge, long-winged owl flying away from us beneath the tree canopy. Fortunately, it landed a short distance away, and I was able to get superb and prolonged views of a legendary bird, that I never thought I would see: Pel's fishing owl.

One of the world's largest owls, this bird has a rufous and ginger tone to its plumage, a huge, rounded head with shaggy feathering, and baleful eyes, making it look like a rather sad lion. Although I knew that Pel's fishing owl can be found across much of sub-Saharan Africa, I was well aware that its usually nocturnal habits mean it is never an easy bird to find. This sighting was a real privilege.

What about the owls I have yet to see? Well, given that my tally so far is just forty of the 250-plus species – fewer than one in six – I have plenty to choose from! But if I were to pick one, it would have to be the species that just manages to top the Eurasian eagle owl as the largest in the world: Blakiston's fish owl (also known as Blakiston's eagle owl).

This elusive bird, confined to the eastern parts of Russia, China and Japan, was not discovered until 1884, when the English ornithologist Henry Seebohm examined a specimen from the Japanese island of Hokkaido. He named it after his fellow-naturalist and explorer Thomas Blakiston, who had 'collected' – i.e. shot – the bird a year earlier.

Having been under the radar for over a century following its discovery, this species gained global fame in 2020, when the US biologist and conservationist Jonathan C. Slaght published the award-winning book *Owls of the Eastern Ice: The Quest to Find and Save the World's Largest Owl*. In its pages, Slaght describes the extraordinary efforts of Russian biologists and conservationists to try to save this magnificent bird – whose entire world population has been estimated as between 1,000 and 1,900 individuals – from sliding towards extinction. A modest man, Slaght has nevertheless been dubbed 'the Jane Goodall of fish owls', after the legendary primatologist. Now that I've read his evocative and passionate book, a trip to northern Japan to try to encounter this legendary owl is at the top of my wish list.

I have enjoyed great good fortune in seeing so many of the world's owls but I am also aware that, like so many other birds, owls are facing major threats to their future. For some species, these may even threaten their continued existence on this planet.

Many kinds of owl – especially, although not exclusively, those species or races confined to small oceanic islands – are currently at risk of extinction, owing to a range of threats including habitat and biodiversity loss, persecution, and of course the climate crisis. Fortunately, many organisations work to actively help and conserve owls, including those dedicated to general bird conservation – such as BirdLife

International, the RSPB, and the BTO – and those focused purely on raptors, such as the Hawk and Owl Trust, Barn Owl Trust and many others across the world.

The Owl Research Institute (ORI), for example, a non-profit organisation founded in 1988 in the US state of Montana by the ecologist and environmental campaigner Denver Holt, has worked tirelessly over recent decades to help threatened North American owls, with its work featured on a wide range of popular natural history television programmes. Holt's knack of communicating the importance of owls to the widest audience has led him, in his June 2022 TED talk, 'Finding Owls', for instance, to imitate the different ways owls communicate with one another at night using unique low-frequency vocalisations – what he memorably describes as 'hoots, toots, trills and hisses'. 'The big ones are hooters and the little ones are tooters.' As he notes, even the youngest children can recognise the calls of owls.

Launched in 1992, the ORI's Snowy Owl Breeding Ecology and Lemming Population Study is centred on a 260 square km (100 square mile) area of Alaska north of the Arctic Circle near Utqiagvik (formerly

Barrow) – the northernmost point of the United States. The study has now been running for over three decades, during which time, it has gathered incredibly useful research on the key relationship between the snowy owl and its main food item, lemmings, tracing the steady decline of both predator and prey. This kind of long-term study is essential if we are to try to reverse the effects of the climate crisis on this charismatic owl.

Another organisation, the Hungry Owl Project, was founded in California in 2001 by Alex Godbe. Its mission – and that of Godbe's most recent venture, All About Owls – is to encourage population growth of these highly effective predators by providing habitat and nest boxes for owls, and ultimately eliminate the need for toxic chemicals, as the owls will kill enough rodents by themselves.

Some groups focus on particular species. The San Diego Zoo burrowing owl program, led by Colleen Wisinski, seeks to counter the continued loss of burrowing owl habitat to urban and suburban development by the clever strategy of squirting white paint around a potential burrowing owl breeding area, to encourage these communally nesting birds to colonise, as they mistake the paint for the droppings of their fellow owls.

By far the best-known campaign to save owls, however, for more than thirty years, has been the one to prevent logging in the old-growth forests where northern spotted owls (a distinctive race of the more widespread spotted owl) live and breed. This close relative of the European tawny owl is native to the Pacific North-west region of the United States, and is considered a crucial 'indicator species'. If they do well, in other words, then so do many other wild creatures; conversely, when they are in decline, other birds and mammals which depend on the forests are also threatened.

The story begins in the late 1980s, when loggers and environmentalists began to come into conflict over the growing destruction of much of the northern spotted owl's unique and valuable habitat, which was being cut down for the forestry industry. In 1990, the US Fish and Wildlife Service (USFWS) listed the species as threatened across a wide swathe of its range, from northern California through Oregon to Washington State. The listing specifically referred to the potential loss of the region's original, old-growth forests as the main threat to the spotted owl's future – especially as it needs large areas of undisturbed habitat in order to successfully breed. The listing effectively stopped all logging in these forests virtually overnight, sparking what became known as the 'spotted owl wars' or 'timber wars'.

The US Congress then suspended those environmental laws, leading campaigners to protest by climbing the trees to stop the loggers cutting them down. Relationships between the two lobbies became very tense indeed, with environmentalists and birders coming into conflict with loggers and the owners of sawmills. The latter claimed that as many as 30,000 jobs would be lost (although later studies reduced this figure considerably, as the industry had long been in decline); the former questioned why industry always seems to take precedence over the natural world. Supporters of the loggers sported bumper sticker slogans of 'Kill a spotted owl – save a logger.'

Though a compromise was eventually found, the conflict left ill-feeling on both sides. To confuse the issue further, another species of owl, the barred owl, had spread into the spotted owl's territory, which appears to have reduced numbers further, as the larger, more dominant species outcompetes its smaller relative. In 2021, the outgoing administration of President Trump removed protection from over three million acres of the Pacific forests. Fortunately, as soon as President Biden came into office, he immediately reversed this decision. Nonetheless, today the population of northern spotted owls is at its lowest ebb since records began: just 2,300 pairs, the majority of them in the state of Oregon. The future of this unique subspecies appears bleak.

One of the most important conundrums facing birders, ornithologists, conservationists and environmentalists the world over is whether we should prioritise the conservation of species or groups of birds – and indeed other wild creatures – that are in some ways 'useful' to us. As the environmental historian Dr Rob Lambert has pointed out, the historical 'journey' we have made alongside birds can, in many ways, be regarded as a slow but steady progress from use to delight: from exploiting birds for food, feathers and other 'products', to delighting in them for their intrinsic beauty or fascinating behaviour. Yet as many have argued, when we assess any wild species for its economic value to us, we in some ways diminish that species, and regress to seeing them simply as something to exploit, or use, in a new way.

But if we do accept that some wild creatures can be useful for human commerce or society, then owls would be high on the list: notably as predators of 'pest species' such as rodents. Studies from California's Napa Valley have shown that barn owls, in particular, have proved highly effective at hunting and killing rodents in the region's famous vineyards, with each owl consuming as many as 3,400 rodents a year. This contributes to a very profitable industry worth some $88 billion (over £70 billion), roughly equivalent to the annual GDP of Sri Lanka.

Encouraging barn owls as natural pest controllers (as opposed to using harmful chemicals such as rodenticides) enables vineyards to promote their product as organic, 'natural' and 'wildlife-friendly', as well as make a major cost saving. The vineyard owners in turn help the owls by putting up nest boxes; one study by Humboldt State University reported that a survey of seventy-five winemakers showed that four out of five of them had done so. Such a simple strategy yields immediate results, as one local ornithologist, John C. Robinson, points out.

'You can literally put a barn owl nest box in the exact location where you think you have a problem with the small mammals, and *voilà*! The owls will start using that area.'

But ultimately, however useful some species of owl have proved to humans, that is not the only reason we should fight to save them. Like all living creatures – and especially the four species I have written about in this 'bird biographies' series, the European robin, Eurasian wren, barn swallow and mute swan – owls have a deep relationship with us through our society, culture, music and literature.

In the end, despite their contrasting – and entirely erroneous – reputations as either cute and cuddly creatures or harbingers of evil, owls are above all, of course, wild birds. And, as I hope this book has proved, they are some of the most curious, mesmerising and fascinating of all.

EPILOGUE

They danced by the light of the moon,
　　The moon,
　　 The moon,
They danced by the light of the moon.

Edward Lear, 'The Owl and the Pussycat' (1870)

On a bright late winter's night, with a full moon shining, I go in search of owls in and around my Somerset village. The moonlight gives me an advantage I don't usually have over the owls: if they are around, I have a better chance of actually seeing them than if it were a cloudy or moonless night. And, of course, if they call, I shall also be able to hear them.

When searching for owls, you need to heighten your senses. So I walk – or, when I need to cover a wider area, cycle – as quietly as I can, taking care not to make any noise that might either frighten or disturb the birds themselves, or simply prevent me from hearing them.

Three species of owl live close to me: a pair of tawny owls nest either towards the back of our garden, or in the tall trees nearby; little owls breed in the orchard next door; barn owls, which prefer more open country, can be found in and around the local farms or – usually at dawn or dusk – quartering the nearby grassy fields. Many of these are neglected or left ungrazed, so have the long vegetation which provides a home for the small rodents such as mice and voles, for which this species hunts.

I start by simply standing outside our door, looking down our long and narrow garden. Learning a lesson from the owls' own anatomy, I mimic their facial disk, which focuses and concentrates sounds, by cupping my hands at the back of my ears. My temperamental inclination

may be to impatience, but I need to take my time: although owls do call regularly after dark, they do not do so constantly.

After twenty minutes or so, during which time I do indeed consider giving up and returning to the brightness, warmth and comfort of our home, I earn my reward: the distant but distinctive hooting of a male tawny owl, closely followed by the eerie *kee-wick* of the female; the classic duet.

I go through the gate at the bottom of our garden and, as my eyes gradually become accustomed to the low light levels, head slowly down the adjacent lane, trying to pinpoint where the birds are calling from. I cross the silage field towards a small group of trees. Sure enough, that is where the birds are hidden, somewhere in the branches.

I listen for a short time, then stroll back up the lane towards the village. Before I get home, I am rewarded once again – this time a slightly higher-pitched, more intense and less disyllabic version of the female tawny's sound. A little owl is calling from somewhere in the orchard, where it nests in some old apple trees. That's good news – they are not here every year. I look forward to hearing, and hopefully seeing, the youngsters when they emerge later in the year and perch on the roof of next door's barns.

Two down, one to go. My third target species – the barn owl – is far less sedentary, and so much less predictable, than its tree-loving cousins. If I am going to come across one, I will probably need to cover a larger distance; the upside being that a hunting barn owl is much easier to see than the other two, especially on a bright moonlit night, when it should stand out because of its pale plumage.

Back home, I get out my road bike and head back down the lane. I decide to do a slow tour of the 3-mile circuit I got to know during the first Covid lockdown in spring 2020, and wrote about in *Skylarks with Rosie*. The eponymous Rosie, our red-fox Labrador, will by now be happily curled up on the sofa next to my wife and daughter, which should make it easier for me to focus on my nightly quest.

I do the four sides of 'the loop', as I call it, with no sign of barn owls – or, indeed, any other living creature. But I have a Plan B: I head northwards, away from the loop, and towards the village of Chapel Allerton, with its medieval church, which dates back to the thirteenth century. I know that barn owls are often seen here: my children have come across them when taking Rosie for a walk, while I once almost ran into one as I returned from the nearby pub, the Wheatsheaf, one summer's evening.

But even though I scan the fields along the road – fields where I sometimes see my favourite local mammals, brown hares – there is still no sign of my quarry, so I turn for home. Two miles later, as I turn the corner by the watery rhyne that runs parallel with the back of our garden, I see a ghostly white shape perched on a gate. It looks briefly at me as if to size me up, then lifts up and floats gently away on silent wings.

Acknowledgements

As always with these bird biographies, I owe a great debt to experts on the species, or in this case the group of them, which are the subject of the book, for their direct or indirect help, knowledge and expertise.

I particularly wish to thank my fellow authors Mark Cocker, Mary Colwell, David Lindo, Mike Toms and Michael J. Warren for allowing me to quote from their writings, and my student on the Bath Spa MA Nature and Travel Writing course, Paul Gamble, for his deep knowledge of the classical world. I would also like to thank the many expert birders and guides who have shown me owls around the world, including Hadoram Shirihai, Killian Mullarney, Hania and Marek Borkowski and Adam Riley.

As ever, thanks to my eagle-eyed (owl-eyed?!) editor Graham Coster, my agent Broo Doherty and her colleague at DHH Literary Agency, David H. Headley, for his enthusiastic support of my books. Huge thanks to my friends Kevin and Donna Cox for once again lending me their Devon cottage as a writing retreat. This book is dedicated to them for their friendship and support over the years.

As always, the team at Square Peg (Penguin Random House) have done a great job on the book: my editor Marianne Tatepo and her assistant Emily Martin; Ryn Gardner in Publicity; Lucy Beresford-Knox in the rights team; production controllers Eoin Dunne and Konrad Kirkham, and Lily Richards and Amelia Tolley in design, who also found the lovely cover image by Simon Turvey.

And finally, to Amy Hall, who did such a brilliant job researching the book, discovering fascinating stories, facts and figures about the world's owls.

List of Illustrations

p. 23 'Long-eared Owl' from *The Observer's Book of British Birds* by S. Vere Benson (1938) © Frederick Warne & Co Ltd.

p. 24 'Close-up of the Skull of an Owl' © NPL – DeA Picture Library / Bridgeman Images.

p. 25 'Owl Feathers' from *A Practical Handbook of British Birds* by H. F. Witherby, Rev. F.C.R. Jourdain, Norman F. Ticehurst and Bernard W. Tucker (1938–41) © Biodiversity Heritage Library, courtesy of Smithsonian Libraries.

p. 27 *'Bubo bubo'*, plate 30 from *The Birds of Great Britain, Vol. 1* by John Gould (1873, hand-coloured lithograph) © Natural History Museum, London / Bridgeman Images.

p. 30 'Malle Babbe' ('Witch of Haarlem') by Frans Hals (1633–5, oil on canvas) @ NPL – DeA Picture Library / Bridgeman Images.

p. 38 'The Enchanted Owl' by Kenojuak Ashevak (1960, stonecut on paper) © Art Gallery of Ontario / Gift of Samuel and Esther Sarick (Toronto, 2002) / Bridgeman Images.

p. 41 'Judge and Jury Owls' by Louis Wain (1892) © Mary Evans Picture Library.

p. 42 'Dancing Along the Shore' by Leonard Leslie Brooke from *The Owl and the Pussycat* by Edward Lear (1922) © Mary Evans / Grenville Collins Postcard Collection.

p. 46 'Tawny, Brown or Wood-Owl' from *Coloured Figures of the Birds of the British Islands, Vol. 1*, by R. H. Porter (1885–97) © Biodiversity Heritage Library, courtesy of Smithsonian Libraries.

p. 50 'The Tawny Owl' from *The Manual of British Birds* by Howard Saunders (1927) © Gurney and Jackbon.

p. 54 'Tawny Owl' from *Birds of Britain* by A. and C. Black (1907) © Biodiversity Heritage Library, courtesy of Smithsonian Libraries.

p. 56 'Owl Eggs' from *A History of British Birds* by R. H. Porter (1883–5) © Biodiversity Heritage Library, courtesy of Smithsonian Libraries.

p. 103 'Little Owl' by F. W. Frohawk from *British Birds with their Nests and Eggs* by Rev. Murray A. Mathew (1896).

p. 110 'Long-eared Owls and Short-eared Owls' from *The Oxford Book of Birds* by Bruce Campbell (1964) © Oxford University Press, 1964.

p. 114 'Vlerk van een Ransuil' by Balthasar Meisner (1898, pencil and water-colour ink) © Gift of M.C.J.F. Meissner, Amsterdam / Rijksmuseum.

p. 115 'Short-eared Owl' from *Coloured Figures of the Birds of the British Islands, Vol. 1*, by R. H. Porter (1885–97) © Biodiversity Heritage Library, courtesy of Smithsonian Libraries.

p. 116 'Owl Feathers' from *A Practical Handbook of British Birds* by H. F. Witherby, Rev. F.C.R. Jourdain, Norman F. Ticehurst and Bernard W. Tucker (1938–41) © Biodiversity Heritage Library, courtesy of Smithsonian Libraries.

p. 118 'Plate XXIII – Short-eared Owl' from *Birds of Village and Field* by Florence A. Merriam (1898) © Biodiversity Heritage Library, courtesy of Smithsonian Libraries.

p. 120 'Short-eared Owl' from *British Birds in their Haunts* by C. A. Johns (1922) © Biodiversity Heritage Library, courtesy of Smithsonian Libraries.

p. 123 'Long-eared Owl' from *Birds of Britain* by A. and C. Black (1907) © Biodiversity Heritage Library, courtesy of Smithsonian Libraries.

p. 124 'Long-eared Owl' by F. W. Frohawk from *British Birds with their Nests and Eggs* by Rev. Murray A Mathew (1896).

p. 126 'Long-eared Owl' from *The Bird-life of London* by W. Heinemann (1909) © Biodiversity Heritage Library, courtesy of Smithsonian Libraries.

p. 128 'Long-eared Owl' from *The Manual of British Birds* by Howard Saunders © Gurney and Jackbon 1927.

p. 130 'Hieroglyphic Relief Depicting Consonant Sound for 'm' (Owl)' (no known date, carving from the Temple of Hatshepsut) © Tarker / Bridgeman Images.

p. 130 'Long-eared Owl' from *Coloured Illustrations of British birds, and their Eggs* by G. W. Nickisson (1842–50) © Biodiversity Heritage Library, courtesy of Smithsonian Libraries.

p. 133 '*Brachyotus Palustris*, plate' from *The Birds of Great Britain* by John Gould (1862–73) © Bridgeman images.

p. 134 'Snowy Owl' from *Coloured Illustrations of British birds, and their Eggs* by G. W. Nickisson (1842–50) © Biodiversity Heritage Library, courtesy of Smithsonian Libraries.

p. 139 '*Nyctea Nivea*', plate from *The Birds of Great Britain* by John Gould (1862–73) © Bridgeman Images.

p. 140 'Snowy Owl', plate from *Selby's Illustrations of British Ornithology* by Prideau John Selby (1819–39) © Bridgeman Images.

p. 143 'Snowy Owl' from *Coloured Figures of the Birds of the British Islands, Vol. 1*, by R. H. Porter (1885–97) © Biodiversity Heritage Library, courtesy of Smithsonian Libraries.

p. 145 'Snowy Owl' by F. W. Frohawk from *British Birds with their Nests and Eggs* by Rev. Murray A. Mathew (1896).

p. 150 'Snowy Owl' by Robert Havell Junior from *Birds of America* by James John Audubon (1831, coloured engraving) © Bridgeman Images.

p. 155 '*Nyctea scandiaca* / Schnee-Eule / Snowy Owl' from *Naturgeschichte der Vogel Mittel-Europas* by Johann Andreas Naumann (1896–1905) © British Library Board, all rights reserved / Bridgeman Images.

p. 156 'Eagle Owl' from *Coloured Figures of the Birds of the British Islands, Vol. 1*, by R. H. Porter (1885–97) © Biodiversity Heritage Library, courtesy of Smithsonian Libraries.

p. 162 'Eagle Owl' by F. W. Frohawk from *British Birds with their Nests and Eggs* by Rev. Murray A. Mathew (1896).

p. 165 'Eagle Owl (*Bubo Ignavus*)' by John Gerard Keulemans from *A History of the Birds of Europe, including all the species inhabiting the Western Palaearctic Region* by Henry Eeles Dresser (1842–1912, hand-coloured engraving) © Christie's Images / Bridgeman Images.

p. 167 'Eagle Owl' from *A History of British Birds, Indigenous and Migratory, Vol. 3* by William Macgillivray (1840).

p. 170 'Owl Mocked by Small Birds' by Kawanabe Kyōsai (*c.* 1997, ink and colour on silk) © Charles Stewart Smith Collection, Gift of Mrs Charles Stewart Smith, Charles Stewart Smith Jr and Howard Caswell Smith, in memory of Charles Stewart Smith (1914) / The Met Museum.

p. 175 '*Athene cunicularia, Athene noctua, Glaucidium gnoma, Asio flammeus,* plate 432' by Robert Havell Junior from *Birds of America* by James John Audubon (1831, coloured engraving) ©Bridgeman Images.

p. 178 'The Fennec Fox and Eagle Owl' by Eric Tansley (1965) © Look and Learn / Bridgeman Images.

p. 181 Spread from *Owls from Natural History of the Animal Kingdom for the Use of Young People* by E. & J. B. Young and Co. (1889) © Biodiversity Heritage Library, courtesy of Smithsonian Libraries.

p. 186 'Full Moon' by Robert Gillmor (no known date, linocut print) © Mary Evans Picture Library.

p. 190 '*Vier steenuilen en twee Torenvalken Dierstudies*' by Theo van Hoytema (1898, print) © Rijksmuseum.

p. 192 'Barn Owl' by Eleanor Fein (2012, painting) © Eleanor Fein, all rights reserved (2023) / Bridgeman Images.